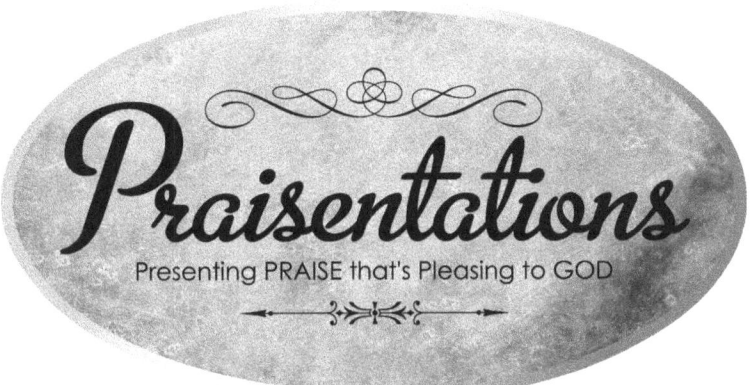

Dr. Charlene Nelson

WriteHouse Publishing
Washington, DC

Copyright © 1999/ 2015 – Charlene Nelson

WriteHouse Publishing – All Rights Reserved

Scripture quotations taken from King James, the Living Bible, Holman Christian Standard, New Living & New International version of the Bible.

ISBN: 069242346X

ISBN-13: 978-0692423462

DEDICATION

To the Triune GOD:
my foundation, my focus and my future

ABOUT THE AUTHOR

Pastor Charlene Nelson

When you experience the ministry of the Lord Jesus Christ through Pastor Charlene Scott, you witness the hand of God in her life. Charlene sang her first song at 3, accepted Jesus at the tender age of 11, made her first international ministry trip at 14, was ordained a youth pastor at 16 and has been joyfully serving God ever since. She offers the message of Christ through a pure and powerful delivery that captivates every listener. Fulfilling her sacred call as pastor/teacher of *Build Forward Missions*, Charlene is in constant demand to bring sound instruction concerning the mandate, *"Thy kingdom come. Thy will be done in earth, as it is in heaven."*

Build Forward Missions is an effective ministry that impacts countless thousands throughout the world in covenant with innovative leaders, Elliott & Michelle Uchiyama. Committed to four key areas: 1) demonstrating the love of God; 2) fervent intercession; 3) witnessing to those seeking answers; 4) renewing faith in the living Savior. During critical historical events the past 14 years, this work has served the White House, Congress, the Military and many mainstream businesses/organizations in their desire to bring America to a place of continual *reverence for God*. *Build Forward Missions* works in partnership with several non-profits in serving, educating and developing communities in the Washington Metropolitan area.

Charlene exuberantly shares love, life and business with her husband, *Dale* who describes his wife as a 'Kingdom Architect' purposefully creating ways to build people up.

Pastor Charlene Scott administers the Word of God with joy, substance, revelation and a prophetic release. Regarded as a 'pastor in the marketplace' she is an author/publisher, speaker, business owner, producer and master coach. Charlene's business dynamic is fortified with immense experience and knowledge; successfully proven for over 29 years. Valuable because of its useful practicality, she has created a book/training series, "GET THE LIFE YOU WANT" which assists individuals, businesses and audiences worldwide in tackling real-life challenges with "doable" strategies. *Build Forward* also shares a timely format through an international radio show, "Focus and Go" and with an emphasis on Christian living/ministry, "Enjoy JESUS with Pastor Cee."

The Lord has gone before Pastor Scott with grace and favor, yet, her humble and direct spirit helps us to return any recognition and attention back to a faithful God whose love is everlasting.

PRAISENTATIONS

Presenting PRAISE that's Pleasing to GOD

Hebrews 13:15-16

"With Jesus' help we will continually offer our sacrifice of PRAISE to GOD by telling others of the glory of His name. Don't forget to do good and to share what you have with those in need, for such sacrifices are very pleasing to Him."

Dr. Charlene Nelson

Let PRAISE GUIDE your way…

CONTENTS

Introduction and Purpose 1
Part One: WHY PRAISE & WORSHIP 3
Part Two: PRAISE 9
   Born to Praise 12
   Only God Holds Your Destiny 17
   Praise is the Sustainer of Every Prayer 20
   Stop Apologizing for Being Blessed 24

Part Three: WORSHIP 27
   The Process of Worship 31
   The Throne Room Experience 34
   How Ya' Livin' 37
   His Goodness, My Reference 40

Part Four: THE BODY OF CHRIST 43
   Corporate Gatherings 44
   Build Up What's Torn Down 47
   Thank You for Remembering Us 50
   Get Ready to Be a Blessing 52

Part Five: THE DEEP CALLETH UNTO THE DEEP............57
  A Sacred Trust 59
  Seven Fruits of Necessity 60
  My Tow Truck Theory 62
  Look In, Line Up, Let Loose 65
  I'll Take You There – The Worship Leader's Decree 68
  The Intimacy of Rehearsal 72
  The Continued Lesson...79
  You Are Working for the Lord Aren't You 81

Part Six: PRECEPT upon PRECEPT, LINE upon LINE.........85
  And They Were One 87
  Somebody Needs You 89
  The T.E.A.M. Acronym 95
  Without Order There Will Be No Anointing 96
  Attributes Of Effectiveness For Praise &
  Worship Ministry 99
  Is That the Same Mouth You Use to Give Him Praise......101
  A Commitment to Study..104
  A Visual Transformation:
  From Stage Presence to Praise Presence 107

Part Seven: I MUST SING THE LORD'S SONG................109
  What Kind of Song Are You Singing 110
  Guidelines for Praise & Worship Song Selection 114
  A Fresh Revelation for a Standard Principle......................115

THE CONCLUSION 119
   I Don't Need Any Proof (Your Word Is
   Enough for Me) 120
   Expect Nothing but Victory..123

As we continue in "Praisentations" we will discover truths and challenges that are presented to awaken our spirit to the need for a life of Praise & Worship and not just moments of traditions or rituals. Each chapter will have supportive topics that explore in great depth the main subject of the featured section. The compilation of each chapter has been prayerfully cultivated to provide further insight and understanding on our main theme of Praise & Worship.

God bless you on your journey…

INTRODUCTION AND PURPOSE

My primary intent is to educate and edify the body of Christ on the purpose, principles, and power found in a life of Praise & Worship. Our objective is to provide guidance based on scripture and scripture alone. This manual has been birthed out of necessity, to serve as a source of reference in an area that is critical to every Believer. Many accept Jesus as their personal Savior but never know Him personally, which is why I believe the church has been working under a handicap. So many of our pastors have become weary because they're carrying a bunch of sheep with broken legs, (so to speak); sheep that will not seek God for themselves. Now, I understand that sheep can not survive without the protective care of a trustworthy shepherd but a herd in which every third sheep has a broken leg that does not heal would eventually paralyze the ability of the shepherd to administer care and guidance to the flock as a whole. This will ultimately ruin the purpose of that gathered flock, (as we've witnessed too many times to mention). As the saying goes, "You can lead a [sheep] to water but you can't make him drink." I've come to the knowledge that when you begin to hunger and thirst after the Lord, He loves you like you're the only one He's loving. The blessed privilege of being one with Christ is made available to all who will believe and receive Him, not just a few. Jesus said, **"I am the Door; anyone who enters in through Me will be saved (will live). He will come in and he will go out [freely], and will find pasture. The thief comes only in order to steal and kill and destroy. I came that they might have *and* enjoy**

life, and have it in abundance (to the full, till it overflows.)" John 10:9-10 (The Amplified Bible).

The Word of God has *all the answers* to every question, however, those answers may come through various means, such as unadulterated teaching and preaching; scriptural study and application; divine revelation or daily experiences as we walk with the Lord. Whatever the means, we must get back to doing things God's way and that is in essence what this Praise & Worship Manual is all about. According to the instruction and wisdom of God through our Lord Jesus Christ, we have developed a practical guidebook that is easy to read but rich in content; designed for all Believers, assistance for leaders, and support for pastors.

My earnest prayer is the Lord meet every need He had in mind when He spoke this ministry and this book into existence.

WHY PRAISE & WORSHIP?

"Praise & Worship is GOD'S Divine Order which the church has tried to make <u>optional</u>."

The church is in a state of emergency! 1) From the standpoint of getting to the place where we function as a 'whole' healthy body of the Lord Jesus Christ and 2) We've come to a critical point in God's call for revival, restoration, and fruitfulness. Without question, there is an urgent need for *real* Praise & *true* Worship. Yes, we quote "Let ever thing that hath breath Praise the Lord" in relation to Praise and we quote, "But the hour cometh, and now is, when the true Worshippers shall Worship the Father in spirit and in truth" in relation to Worship. Yet, the Lord is *still seeking* that people; that living, breathing tabernacle. That sanctuary found in the spirit of true Believers where the holiness of God may dwell.

PRAISE & WORSHIP is by divine order. It is a directive from God. The only way we are to know God, His son, Jesus and the person of the Holy Spirit is through the Word. The Lord has very specific desires and standards for us to live by. We have spent entirely too much precious time discussing, arguing and misinterpreting the pure essence of God's intent and purpose concerning Praise & Worship. Praise & Worship was established at the throne of God not under the cultural adaptations of doctrinal teachings. A good example of this is when I taught on Praise & Worship at a church where the membership was comprised of those of Asian ethnicity (they were independent). One of the questions posed to me was, "How can we truly express what we feel while in the presence of God when we are a naturally passive people and are taught to exemplify dignity at all times?" These precious souls were prisoners of their heritage. The Word of God declares that once we give our lives to Jesus we are of a new lineage. **II Corinthians 5:17** says, "Therefore if any man be in Christ, he is a new creature: old things are passed away; behold, all things are become new." The question itself signifies there was something beyond their normal thinking and natural behavior leading them to a place they were unfamiliar with. This is when you need the Holy Spirit to be your guide. The things of God can not be obtained through our human understanding. Once we get to this point, our humanity (reasoning mind) is in the way. The Bible says, *"So then they that are in the flesh cannot please God. But ye are not in the flesh, but in the Spirit, if so be that the Spirit of God dwell in you. Now if any man have not the Spirit of Christ, he is none of His."* (**Romans 8:8-9**) We try to reason our way out of obeying the Lord. Thus, we must guard ourselves against what I call, 'Preoccupied Praise and Wandering Worship.' We have to be altogether present, mind, body, soul and spirit. Let's learn how to enclose our minds and focus on Jesus so that the Holy Ghost of God can grab hold and bless us. We must literally train ourselves to seize the moment. Not only in our private time with the Lord but as important during corporate Praise & Worship, the time we've set aside to come together as the body of Christ. We're often guilty of having our physical bodies present but our minds are far from Jesus. He speaks of this in **Matthew 15:8-9** (NLT), *"These people honor me with their lips, but their hearts are far from me. Their worship is a farce, for they teach man-made ideas as commands of God."* And because we can not begin to fathom the mind of God we want to remain open, attentive, and available to His 'right now' move. Our half-hearted, irregular Praise & Worship will hinder the spontaneity of the Spirit. The Lord knows exactly what we need at that time but we must first present ourselves to Him in a way that pleases Him. Then the Holy Spirit will usher us to His loving embrace. How many of us have chased the pastor/preacher after service? Or called them when we got home? How many of us go to counseling sessions over and over again for the same things? Pastors are committed as under shepherds, they can even speak to God on our behalf but *they can not live our lives for us.* God has entrusted pastors to provide an environment where the Lord can have His way, where refuge and peace are a priority, where joy and love reside. Then, once we are led to His strong arm and loving embrace, we will find what we need is there. Praise & Worship disciplines us to go to God *first*. Whatever we need can be found in His presence. *"Thou wilt shew me the path of life: in thy presence is fullness of joy; at thy right hand are pleasures for evermore."* (**Psalm 16:11**)

That's why we should pray daily for the Lord to open up our spirit to the truths of His Word. If every Believer were empowered with the Word of God and putting that Word into practice daily we would be able to keep the enemy in his place, which is under our feet. *"And the Lord shall make thee the head, and not the tail; and thou shalt be above only, and thou shalt not be beneath; if that thou hearken unto the commandments of the Lord thy God, which I command thee this day, to observe and to do them."* (**Deuteronomy 28:13**). In order to do what God's Word says, we must know what God's Word says. When you prepare for your worship time (public or private) have your Bible with you. The Bible is direct revelation and divine inspiration straight from the heart of God. **II Timothy 3:16-17** says, *"All scripture is given by inspiration of God, and is profitable for doctrine, for reproof, for correction, for instruction in righteousness: That the man of God may be perfect, thoroughly furnished unto all good works."* The Living Bible says it this way, *"The whole Bible was given to us by inspiration from God and is useful to teach us what is true and to make us realize what is wrong in our lives; it straightens us out and helps us to do what is right. It is God's way of making us well prepared at every point, fully equipped to do good to everyone."* Many people try to establish their Praise & Worship outside of the Word, which results in an unprepared, unequipped child of God who needs to be 'recalled.' Then, there are some that only want to accept God's Word in part. It offends God when we decide to adhere to His Word partially, to advocate only those scriptures that match our preferences, upbringing, and tastes. For example, some refuse to dance before the Lord, some won't believe to speak in tongues and some are bothered by the way other people express themselves to God. I've learned one vein of truth that remains consistent throughout my assignment of teaching on Praise & Worship, those that are most rebellious to this mandate do not know the Word of God and for those that do know, this is double indemnity because they are deliberately living in disobedience. What makes you think He will welcome you into His eternal glory when you won't welcome Him in right now? Stop letting your pride hinder your Praise. On many occasions in the Bible, God highlighted examples of true Praise so we could see the results and believe Him to do the same for us.

Praise & Worship is not only an honor and privilege but it's a valuable asset in the life of every Believer. It is one of the tools the Lord has provided to cover us from the attacks of the enemy.

Praise & Worship has a two-fold <u>function</u>:

<u>Function 1</u>: It draws us to the One who made us and the reason we are made. *"But ye are a chosen generation, a royal priesthood, an holy nation, a peculiar people; that ye should shew forth the praises of Him who hath called you out of darkness into His marvelous light."* **(I Peter 2:9)**

<u>Function 2</u>: As a tool to combat the ongoing assault of Satan.

"For the weapons of our warfare are not carnal, but mighty through God to the pulling down of strongholds." **(II Corinthians 10:4)**

It is critical then that we learn our place in the Kingdom and put these tools in full operation in God's provision to us. So, these functions in full operation yield God-centered results:

Result 1: As we were created to bless God, we begin to live in the power of the knowledge of Whose/who we are.

Result 2: We are shielded against the wiles of the enemy.

God delights in us as we delight in Him.

PRAISE

"A Bad Day is a Good Day to give GOD PRAISE!"

PRAISE

Praise is a vital characteristic in the life of God's people. Praise is a demonstration of appreciation and adoration to God and may be accompanied by expressions of joy. Believers offer praise to the Father in acknowledgement of His existence, all that He is and for what He has done. God's people have a responsibility, an obligation to praise God. We offer praise both individually and collectively. We must sincerely desire that our lives and actions bring praise to God, not to ourselves. **Psalm 115 vs. 1** says, *"Not unto us, O Lord, not unto us, but unto thy name give glory, for thy mercy, and for thy truth's sake."* A faithful life of praise should also cause others to give Him praise. The act of Praise & Worship is supported and displayed throughout the scriptures.

> **Praise and Worship in their varied forms, are mentioned far more than any other of our basic Biblical principles. Shouting is listed 65 times; Thanksgiving – 135 times; Singing – 287 times; Rejoicing – 288 times; and Playing Musical Instruments – 317 times. The command "Praise!" occurs 332 times in the Bible, while the extended command, "Praise the Lord" is listed an additional 50 times.*

*Worship as David Lived it – Judson Cornwall/Revival Press

We have very explicit instructions from the Lord to acknowledge, honor, and serve Him through the disciplines of Praise & Worship. Many are afraid of what I call 'Hands on Praise' which is participating rather than being mere spectators. In any given setting those gathered can come from all ends of the spectrum; different locations, different backgrounds, different references and the list goes on and on but none of these things should keep us from giving God the praise He deserves. *"It is a good thing to give thanks unto the Lord and to sing praises unto thy name, O most High."* (**Psalm 92:1**) *"Behold, how good and how pleasant it is for brethren to dwell together in unity!"* (**Psalm 133:1**) Praise is in fact the entry-way to Worship but is not a trivial matter. God is a God of order and you can not haphazardly fling yourself at Him and expect Him to respond. How do we approach Him? **Psalm 100:2** says, *"Serve the Lord with gladness: come before His presence with singing."* Start by becoming a servant with joy in your heart. It amazes me that any scripture which requires an effort on our part is very often overlooked. How many times have we gone to the house of God expecting a blessing when we know our lifestyles are a mess? "The Lord sits high and He looks low." Some of us must think He can only see us when we're in church – Wake Up! One of the main benefits of a consistent life of Praise is a *constant awareness of His presence*, not in a microscopic sense. There's true spiritual enlightenment brought forth out of a life of genuine praise. You begin to see God in the little things, you develop a thirst for God, and you begin to live with a grateful heart not a greedy spirit. We must seek God's heart not just His hand. Don't take God's goodness for granted – you <u>owe</u> Him a Praise!

BORN TO PRAISE

Psalm 71:5-8 (The Amplified Bible) says, *"For You are my hope; O Lord God, You are my trust from my youth and the source of my confidence. Upon You have I leaned and relied from birth; You are He Who took me from my mother's womb and You have been my benefactor (meaning the One who has been good) from that day. My praise is continually of You. I am as a wonder and surprise to many, but You are my strong refuge. My mouth shall be filled with Your praise and with Your honor all the day."*

This psalm is attributed to David. We've all heard the story of David. The little shepherd boy who killed a giant and went on to become the king of Israel. When the Lord sent Samuel to go find and anoint the next king, Samuel went to the house of Jesse (David's father). David was the youngest of eight boys. When Samuel got to the house, David was no where around. But after Samuel had been introduced to the other seven brothers (not even knowing about David) he asked, "Are here all thy children?" And David's father said, "No, there is the youngest who is not here." Samuel said, "Go and get him, we can not sit down until he comes." That must have blown everybody's mind who was present in the house. Little David; he was the least (or so it appeared) of all. Yet, he was God's choice. Not only was David anointed king during that time but he is still considered to be the father of Praise & Worship. The praiser of Praisers. Dancing David. Singing/Songwriting David. Harp playing David. Lion, Bear, Giant slaying David. David, a man after God's own heart. But wait…isn't this the same David that committed adultery and murder – Yes it is. My brother, my sister, this is where we gain hope. I've always loved how God developed the Word in that He just didn't write all the good stuff and leave out the bad; God thought it crucial to give present things as they were. David sinned against God. And as people often do 'rate' sin, murder is considered one of the worst and most unforgivable. David is a real example of the mercy and grace of God. In spite of his failures, David knew undoubtedly he was born to praise. He got caught up in his lust and desires, messed up his life and Bathsheba's, took the life of her devoted husband and had the destiny of an entire nation in his hands. Yet, David didn't allow his sin to beat him down forever. He REPENTED and asked God's forgiveness. God not only forgave him but guess what, KING JESUS came from the line of David. What a tremendous honor!

<u>GOD wants you to know today</u>:

- No matter who your mother and father is (whether you know them or not, whether you have them or not)
- No matter what circumstances you are living with/under
- No matter how many times your heart has been broken
- No matter who has abused or misused you
- No matter who you've hurt, used or abused
- No matter what anyone has said to you or about you that does not line up with the Word of God
- No matter what your current state is
- No matter what you have or don't have, who you know or don't know
- No matter how bad you've failed or how many times you've failed

Remember…**YOU WERE BORN TO PRAISE!**

Even if you have made a mess of your life:

- Ruined the trust of everybody who has tried to help you
- Lied, stolen, gotten bad grades
- Disappointed your parents, loved ones and friends
- Been sexually active, not sure of your God-given sexual identity
- Had a baby or babies (outside of marriage)
- Had an abortion
- Fathered a child or children you don't take care of
- Belong to a gang, been in a detention center or prison
- Or committed the unmentionable sin like David; murdered someone

Know that we are praying with you right now…THERE IS HOPE IN JESUS CHRIST! DON'T GIVE UP ON YOURSELF! YOU WERE BORN TO PRAISE! BORN TO GIVE GOD GLORY! The devil wants you to give up before GOD can show you your future in HIM. Don't be defeated before you really get started. Don't let devastation destroy you. What you have to know is God is faithful and just to forgive. God doesn't hang things over your head once you have *sincerely* **repented**. As a song I love says, "*He's already forgotten what we can't forget.*" The key is to repent. Repent and GET TO PRAISING! The Holy Spirit will guide you in working on those things that do not please God. With the aid of the Holy Spirit and others, you can get your life in order and keep it in order. Praise will not only get you out of a mess, it will keep you mindful of how much you really need God. It's a miracle you are here. The devil is waging an attack on you as never before, he wants to kill you before you realize WHOSE you are. YOU BELONG TO GOD. CREATED FOR HIS GLORY. You have a will, you have a choice, take your life back – no longer allow the enemy to run rip shod over you.

<u>Because of the grace of our Lord, you have</u>:

- A right to salvation
- A right to the love of family and friends
- A right to have dignity and self-respect
- The right to use the gifts God gave you

<u>Your gifts should be used for Kingdom building</u>:

- If you have talent, dedicate it to the glory of God.
- If you're athletic, play for God.
- If you're musical, give your song to God.
- If you're intelligent, use your brains for God.
- If you have the gift of helps, help somebody for God.

Whatever you've been blessed to do, do it as unto God.

Open up to those who have been through and made it – they can help you make it. And like David you can say, God, my hope is in You. I'm gonna trust You, it's been You that has protected me since I was born. I will always praise You. I want my life to be an example to many. I want them to be amazed at what You've done for me. Lord, You've kept me, You've defended me. Every day, all day long, I will praise You and give You glory. I know it now…I was BORN TO PRAISE! Begin to praise Him right now…

ONLY GOD HOLDS YOUR DESTINY

In the day in which we live it's tempting to measure our success (or lack thereof) by the accomplishments of another. If we fair well in our estimation we can even feel we've arrived based on who we know or the position we hold. It is especially disheartening to see this happening in the house of God, just like the secular world there are many games being played in order to climb up 'corporate' ladder. While climbing up this ladder many of the "saints" have disobeyed the commandments of God, hurt and destroyed others, forsaken their families and forgotten the very reason for being born again: to glorify the Lord Jesus Christ.

This is a pleasant and joyful reminder: ONLY GOD HOLDS YOUR DESTINY! We must show God how much we trust Him by putting our lives totally in His hands. Yes, it's true we are helpers one of another but that's all we are. You don't give the right that only Christ should have to another person; He IS the author and finisher of our faith. Only He knows the blueprint fashioned for us and exactly how we are to get there. So many of us have allowed others to make us feel indebted to them and thus become tied into a commitment God is not in agreement with. No matter who has helped us along the way (and we should thank God for them) God gets all the glory! You want to walk by faith such that only God can take the credit for who you are and any blessed work done through you.

Destiny ownership is a vital aspect of your walk with God, a privilege that only God should have in your life. When the enemy tries to entice you to go overboard in your relationships / commitments / trusts in others; put your life back into God's hands. Whenever the enemy has you seeking the advice of men above the voice of God; it's time to put your life back into God's hands. When you trust in the patterns of this world more than the direction of God, you've got to grab hold of these scriptures and put your life back into God's hands…willingly, joyfully.

Jeremiah 1:5 (a & b), *"Before I formed thee in the belly I knew thee; and before thou camest forth out of the womb I sanctified thee…"* This scripture amazes me. God knew me before I got here and set me apart to do His will before I came out of my mother's womb. You too! He has plans for us. Special assignments we are to fulfill while here on earth. The enemy's job is to get us preoccupied with a different agenda than God's; to have us busying ourselves with people and things that'll take you away from your true calling. Trust in the One who made you. His way is perfect.

Psalm 75:6-7, *"For promotion cometh neither from the east, nor from the west, nor from the south. But God is the judge: He putteth down one, and setteth up another."* Why are we compromising our spiritual principles to get in good with someone? Even if a pastor places you in a ministry or an auxiliary, it is our prayer they were led by God and if that be the case be assured God has prepared you for that responsibility and God will keep you. Don't establish a rapport with a leader for selfish motives. Only what you do for Christ will last. If we are walking upright before God, in His time He will promote us. The favor of God is more than all the status and riches of this world.

Galatians 1:10 (NLT), *"Obviously, I'm not trying to win the approval of people, but of God. If pleasing people were my goal, I would not be Christ's servant."* This means if our motive is to impress men, God can not trust us. When the opinions of people matter above the approval of God we can be convinced to do things outside of His blueprint for our lives.

John 12:43, *"For they loved the praise of men more than the praise of God."* A dear friend of mine shared an experience with me I'd like to share with you. He had to do a musicians' clinic and he knew that many of the best in the city were expected to be there. He said he felt so much pressure to do something spectacular because they would not accept anything less. Not to mention some of the other clinicians were some 'big name artists' who could offer him more exposure. He worked, studied and prepared. He did the workshop and (if he might say so) he felt it was the best one he's ever done. But strangely enough no one came to comment or compliment him after it was over. He was very discouraged and even worried. While he was on the way home he heard a small voice say, "How does it feel when I get all the glory!?! Lord, help us not to value the praise of men but earnestly desire to hear you say, **"Well done, my good and faithful servant."**

A life of obedience and contentment stir God to release you to His divine destiny. *Look up, not around.* Let God be God – ONLY HE HOLDS YOUR DESTINY!!!

PRAISE IS THE SUSTAINER OF EVERY PRAYER

The Lord has been instructing me in a very specific area of my discipleship – PRAYER. The last eighteen years have been instruction for a lifelong lesson, a lesson He told me to share with you.

The Bible admonishes us to pray; to value the privilege of being able to communicate with the Father; to pray continually and consistently. *"And He spake a parable unto them to this end, that men ought always to pray, and not to faint."* (**Luke 18:1**) *"Watch ye therefore, and pray always…"* (**Luke 21:36a**) *"Pray without ceasing"* (**I Thessalonians 5:17**) *"I will therefore that men pray every where, lifting up holy hands, without wrath and doubting."* (**I Timothy 2:8**) Prayer keeps us attuned to the mind of God. Its primary purpose is not to be a request line but rather a life line for those that desire to know God intimately and walk with God daily. God has also given us the right to approach the throne of grace boldly, that we may obtain mercy, and find grace to help in time of need (**Hebrews 4:16**). What an encouragement this is. We don't have to tiptoe around the throne. We can pour our hearts and souls out before God without fear. He longs to have us rush to His feet and share our deepest concerns. But it doesn't end there…

After we have sought God in prayer, we've got to learn to release our prayers completely to God with Praise. Praise that follows a fervent prayer says I trust You before I see any evidence of what I've prayed. I'm convinced that You and You alone are able to perform it. Lord God, I'm giving You total control of the outcome of my prayer. I will not check with you periodically to update my original requests according to daily circumstances but instead I will bless You all the more knowing You know what's best for me. This is what God wants but sometimes it is so hard for us to do. Receive and embrace this life-changing principle: ***Praise is the sustainer of every prayer. Sustain means to hold up, to support, to give strength to, to endure, to nourish, to bear up under.*** What wonderful insight to <u>increasing the potency of our prayer life</u>. Let's look to the Word of God for support.

OLD TESTAMENT EXAMPLE

I Samuel 1:2-19 (NLT / selected portions) reads, "Elkanah had two wives, Hannah and Peninnah. Peninnah had children, but Hannah did not. On the days Elkanah presented his sacrifice, he would give portions of the meat to Peninnah and each of her children. And though he loved Hannah, he would give her only one choice portion because the LORD had given her no children. So Peninnah would taunt Hannah and make fun of her because the LORD had kept her from having children. Year after year it was the same—Peninnah would taunt Hannah as they went to the Tabernacle. Each time, Hannah would be reduced to tears and would not even eat. Once after a sacrificial meal at Shiloh, Hannah got up and went to pray. Eli the priest was sitting at his customary place beside the entrance of the Tabernacle. Hannah was in deep anguish, crying bitterly as she prayed to the LORD. And she made this vow: 'O LORD of Heaven's Armies, if you will look upon my sorrow and answer my prayer and give me a son, then I will give him back to you. He will be yours for his entire lifetime, and as a sign that he has been dedicated to the LORD, his hair will never be cut.' As she was praying to the LORD, Eli watched her. Seeing her lips moving but hearing no sound, he thought she had been drinking. 'Must you come here drunk?' he demanded. 'Throw away your wine!' 'Oh no, sir!' she replied. 'I haven't been drinking wine or anything stronger. But I am very discouraged, and I was pouring out my heart to the LORD. Don't think I am a wicked woman! For I have been praying out of great anguish and sorrow.' 'In that case,' Eli said, 'go in peace! May the God of Israel grant the request you have asked of him.' *'Oh, thank you, sir!' she exclaimed. Then she went back and began to eat again, and she was no longer sad*. The entire family got up early the next morning and went to worship the LORD once more. Then they returned home to Ramah. When Elkanah slept with Hannah, the LORD remembered her plea, and in due time she gave birth to a son. She named him Samuel, for she said, 'I asked the LORD for him."

NEW TESTAMENT EXAMPLE

Acts 16: 19-26 (selected portions**)** reads, "And when her masters saw that the hope of their gains was gone, they caught Paul and Silas, and drew them into the marketplace unto the rulers, And brought them to the magistrates, saying, These men being Jews, do exceedingly trouble our city. And when they had laid many stripes upon them, they cast them into prison, charging the jailor to keep them safely. *And at midnight Paul and Silas prayed, and sang praises unto God: and the prisoners heard them.* And suddenly there was a great earthquake, so that the foundations of the prison were shaken: and immediately all the doors were opened, and every one's bands were loosed."

PRESENT DAY EXAMPLE

The Lord had placed on my heart in the spring of 1996 to pray for property to house the ministry. Our staff prayed and the Lord showed us which property He desired for our ministry work. We went through all the legalities and after everything was approved the owner let us know we could move forward in our plans. A week later after we had offered a prayer of thanksgiving and celebrated the blessings of God, the owner called back to tell us he had changed his mind. I was stunned and devastated but I immediately heard the Lord say, *"Just keep thanking Me." That same day, I rode over to the property and sat in the car. I had a private praise service right there in the car. I praised God as I saw us walking around, in full operation, doing the work of the Lord there in the property.* A peace came over my soul such as I had never felt. Two days later the owner called and said, "Ms. Nelson, I want to apologize for putting you through so much, if you still want the property, it's yours." I feel a hallelujah right now. Can God, God can!

PRAISE - apply this discipline to your prayer life and you will experience:

- A whole new level of trust in God
- Peace while you're waiting
- Testimonies that will build your faith

Praise & Worship are the wings that keep our Prayers in flight!

STOP APOLOGIZING FOR BEING BLESSED!!!

It amazes me when it becomes 'obvious' that God is blessing a particular individual, family or group, how some respond. Yes, there are some who genuinely celebrate the goodness of Jesus with you but there are others who question your worthiness or how legitimate the blessing is based on their assessment of who they think you are and where they think you are in your relationship with Christ. That in essence is a very private matter. I have a motto I use quite frequently, *"My PRAISE, My BLESSING, My LIFE is NOT subject to your approval."* What does that mean? You didn't have anything to do with the salvation of my soul; the keeping of my mind; the health in my body; the blessing of my family & friends; the Word that nurtured me; the blood that covered me; the power that protected me – I could go on but I feel God and I need to stop and say, *"Lord, I thank You. I give You all the praise for every miracle, for every blessing, only You could have done this for me."*

Let's look at what the Word has to say about this. David the king of Israel was responsible for making sure the Ark of the Lord was returned, (during that critical time the Ark represented the presence of God. To be before the Ark was to be in God's glory although His presence was not limited to the Ark.) So, it was a sacred moment for the Israelites when the Ark was brought to Jerusalem. However, during the process of bringing it the Lord God wanted the people to be sensitive to His instructions and a soldier was killed for touching the Ark. This troubled David and he became even more cautious in his plans to transport the Ark to their homeland. **II Samuel 6:9-16** (The Living Bible) *"David was now afraid of the Lord and asked, "How can I ever bring the Ark home?" So he decided against taking it into the City of David, but carried it instead to the home of Obededom, who had come from Gath. It remained* *there for three months, and the Lord blessed Obededom and all his household. When David heard this, he brought the Ark to the City of David with a great celebration. After the men who were carrying it had gone six paces, they stopped and waited so that he could sacrifice an ox and fat lamb. And David danced before the Lord with all his might, and was wearing priests' clothing. So Israel brought home the Ark of the Lord with much shouting and blowing of trumpets. But as the procession came into the city, Michal, Saul's daughter, watched from a window and saw king David leaping and dancing before the Lord; and she was filled with contempt for him."* Michal (David's wife), just like many people standing back watching us at a distance, did not understand the significance of the blessing, nor did she care to. She was looking at things from a natural and a carnal perspective. David's motive for going forth in the dance with a spirit of celebration and praise was to acknowledge the King of Glory was coming in – The LORD strong and mighty, the LORD mighty in battle.

When you submit your whole heart to Christ, there are certain disciplines that begin to take place and just like David you dance, shout and rejoice in expectation that the glory of the Lord is your guiding light. You're no longer functioning on your on agenda but trusting in the Lord in every facet of your life. People will misunderstand your motives and they can send a message (verbal or nonverbal) that they are not in agreement with what God is doing *but* <u>the key is GOD is doing it not you and not them</u>. So, their opinions, judgments and accusations are unimportant. If we would just obey God daily, He will handle the results. The only thing that matters is pleasing God and allowing Him to have His way – *all the time*.

Apologies come in many different forms. Sometimes we say I'm sorry; sometimes we send flowers and a card; sometimes we use a more elaborate way to express our regrets and sometimes we simply change our behavior or demeanor to speak for us. How many times have you stopped yourself from testifying about the blessings of God because you knew it would cause people to ignore you or to act jealously towards you? Have you ever had a real praise hemmed up inside because you knew your exuberance would raise questions? Stop Apologizing – Rejoice in Jesus! Celebrate His Goodness! Tell the world how great God is! Remember, true, sincere praise keeps you humble. Straightforward, wholehearted Worship will keep you before the Lord so He can continue to come in. I am what God says I am. I'm Saved, I'm Delivered, I'm Set Free, I'm Anointed, I'm Productive in the Spirit and there's nothing anyone can do about it. I'm not sorry just grateful! I am Blessed and I shall be a Blessing!

WORSHIP

"If you were the only one WORSHIPPING GOD, would He be <u>pleased</u>?"

We are not to downplay the importance of Praise or interrupt the delicate intertwining of the two, Praise & Worship. *Real PRAISE can evolve into True Worship!*

WORSHIP

Worship means you have a fervent, passionate devotion, respect and reverence (fear) for *the* Almighty God. Worship is born out of love. The human being has an innate yearning to worship, but after we accept Christ into our lives we must direct and reserve all of our worship for Jesus. Unbeknown to many Believers they have learned to worship – just not <u>**Jesus *only***</u>. It may be your spouse, your children, your good reputation, whatever it is that you feel you can not live without. Often times it is your material possessions, listen to what the Bible says about this, ***"Their gods are merely manmade things of silver and of gold. And those who make and worship them are just as foolish as their idols are!"*** **(Psalm 115:4 & 5**/TLB) In real, Christ-centered worship we open ourselves up for God to correct spiritually what the world has taught us naturally. We are naturally going to worship something or someone but the Lord Jesus wants us back. Worship goes past the acquaintance of, to a *relationship with*. Worship denotes intimate fellowship. Worship also requires the courage to be naked before the Lord. With praise you can remain on the surface, hang around in the outer court and get quite comfortable at a base level but when you sense your spirit longing for more this is the initial call to worship. Don't ignore it, go beyond what you are accustomed to – answer the call. When this type of spirit-let worship is taking place God not only blesses us but we learn daily how to bless Him. It's an intensely reciprocal bond.

We humble ourselves before God as those who serve, honor, fear (respect), and adore Him. We worship in never ending appreciation of His infinite worth. Yet, Worship is not something grim, dull or cheerless as so many believe. True Worship brings great joy, for it is the enjoyment of God himself. The greater the appreciation Believers have of God's holy character and gracious works, the more they adore and love Him. Once we realize the grace of God and accept the gift of His Son, Jesus, our worship gets to the place where it's almost unspeakable.

Our worship relationship with the Lord requires intricate time, attention and care. Real worship promises to bring real fulfillment and satisfaction, *"But whosoever drinketh of the water that I shall give him shall never thirst; but the water that I shall give him shall be in him a well of water springing up into everlasting life."* (**John 4:14**) We will not reach our ultimate plateau until the age to come, *"For now we see through a glass, darkly; but then face to face: now I know in part; but then shall I know even as also I am known."* (**I Corinthians 13:13**) Every day with Jesus is sweeter than the day before.

Worship is to keep us pure before God. **Psalm 18:26a** says, **"With the pure thou wilt shew thyself pure."** It becomes extremely difficult for the enemy to entice us with the sins of this world or impurities in the community of Believers if we keep our focus on God. He needs a direct line to us if He is to influence us. As the Lord has taught me, let me ask you, "How can you obey God if you don't *know* God?" It then becomes critical that your spirit is aligned with the Spirit of God. **"And Christ lives within you, so even though your body will die because of sin, the Spirit gives you life because you have been made right with God. The Spirit of God, who raised Jesus from the dead, lives in you. And just as God raised Christ Jesus from the dead, He will give life to your mortal bodies by this same Spirit living within you. Therefore, dear brothers and sisters, you have no obligation to do what your sinful nature urges you to do. For if you live by its dictates, you will die. But if through the power of the Spirit you put to death**

the deeds of your sinful nature, you will live. For all who are led by the Spirit of God are children of God. So you have not received a spirit that makes you fearful slaves. Instead, you received God's Spirit when He adopted you as His own children. Now we call Him, "Abba, Father." For His Spirit joins with our spirit to affirm that we are God's children." (Romans 8:10-16) You will never be deceived or misled by the Spirit of God. Jesus said in John 10:27-28, **"My sheep hear my voice, and I know them, and they follow me. And I give unto them eternal life; and they shall never perish, neither shall any man pluck them out of my hand."**

How many Christians are lost or pretending because we simply do not understand how to come into real worship with a living God? You go in church, just like any other environment and do as the 'Romans' do but many pastors and church leaders themselves are victim to the limitations of what they've been exposed to and not the liberating power found through obedience to the Word of God. So, while it is we trust the headship has sought the Lord and the Word in order to properly lead us into God's presence don't become slothful in your own pursuit of Christ. How do we know this is a worship service that will take us to the throne of God? I've surrendered my spirit (daily) to the Spirit of God and therein I can bear witness to the authenticity of the move of God.

Am I participating in something that is grieving God? Are we all emotion and no substance? Do we join heaven in declaring the glory of God or are we just making sounds that heaven does not hear? Any part of our flesh that has not died or is not dying will hinder a free flow of real worship. Once we have received God as our Father, He then looks to see *Himself* in His children. Are you one of His?

THE PROCESS OF WORSHIP

There are specific structural disciplines in the Word of God that must be practiced if we are to reach the throne of God. This will eventually lead to a place of intimate joy and unshakable peace in Jesus, while allowing the Holy Spirit to produce God-directed results in our daily lives. The following four aspects are crucial in the foundation, development and continual pursuit of a God-ordained ministry life of Praise & Worship both individually and corporately:

I. **FOCUS**

    A. On **Whom** we are Worshipping. *"Jesus said unto him, Thou shalt love the Lord thy God with all thy heart, and with all thy soul, and all thy mind. This is the first and great commandment."* (**Matthew 22:37**)

    B. On **Why** we are Worshipping. *"Moreover, because of what Christ has done we have become gifts to God that He delights in, for as part of God's sovereign plan we were chosen from the beginning to be His, and all things happen just as He decided long ago. God's purpose in this was that we should praise God and give glory to Him for doing these mighty things for us, who were the first to trust in Christ."* (**Ephesians 1:11-12**/TLB)

    C. On **When** we are to Worship. *"I WILL bless the Lord at all times: His praise shall continually be in my mouth."* (**Psalm 34:1**)

II. **FELLOWSHIP** (through Kinship)

    A. With God. *"The Spirit itself beareth witness with our spirit, that we are the children of God."* (**Romans 8:16**)

1. We become a reflection of His character. *"Sanctify yourselves therefore, and be ye holy: for I am the Lord your God."* (**Leviticus 20:7**)

2. We have the honor of being in His company. *"Surely the righteous shall give thanks unto thy name: the upright shall dwell in thy presence."* (**Psalm 140:13**)

3. We receive the authority to claim His promises to us. *"If ye abide in me, and my words abide in you, ye shall ask what ye will, and it shall be done unto you."* (**Matthew 7:7**)

B. Within the Body of Christ. *"Behold, how good and pleasant it is for brethren to dwell together in unity."* (**Psalms 133:1**)

III. **FREEDOM**

A. To declare (and maintain) victory over sin and death. *"Standfast therefore in the liberty wherewith Christ hath made you free, and be not entangled again with the yoke of bondage."* (**Galatians 5:1**)

B. To walk in the newness of life. *"If the Son therefore shall make you free, ye shall be free indeed."* (**John 8:36**)

C. To experience the move of God. *"Now the Lord is that Spirit: and where the Spirit of the Lord is, there is liberty."* (**II Corinthians 3:17**)

IV. **FULFILLMENT**

A. For every possible void / From all worldly distractions. *"For He satisfieth the longing soul, and filleth the hungry soul with goodness."* (**Psalms 107:9**)

B. To claim ownership/access as a joint heir. *"And if children, then heirs; heirs of God, and joint-heirs with Christ; if so be that we suffer with Him, that we may also be glorified together."* (**Romans 8:17**) *"The earth is the Lord's and the fullness thereof; the world, and they that dwell therein."* (**Psalms 24:1**)

C. For peace that passes all understanding. *"Thou wilt shew me the path of life: in thy presence is fullness of joy; at thy right hand there are pleasures for evermore."* (**Psalms 16:11**)

Dr. Charlene Nelson

A THRONE ROOM EXPERIENCE

Isaiah 6 is one of the most profound passages in the Bible. Although I'm familiar with this chapter God gave me revelation which has enriched my constant desire to stay before the Throne at the feet of Jesus. Now, let's explore this chapter in greater depth so we can share the glory.

Isaiah 6:1-4 (TLB), *"In the year that king Uzziah died I saw also the Lord sitting upon a throne, high and lifted up, and His train filled the temple. Above it stood the seraphims: each one had six wings. With twain he covered his face; with twain he covered his feet, and with twain he did fly. And one cried unto another, and said, Holy, holy, holy, is the Lord of hosts; the whole earth is full of His glory. And the posts of the door moved at the voice of him that cried, and the house was filled with smoke."*

Most of us look past the very first clause of this passage, *"In the year that king Uzziah died..."* God told me to research the life of king Uzziah. Uzziah was placed over the throne of Judah (Praise) at the age of 16. During his early years he relied on the wisdom of Zechariah who instructed him in the fear of God but it was Uzziah's pride in his own considerable accomplishments that led to his undoing. He had a lengthy reign from approximately 783 to 742 B.C. and came into power at a particularly troubled time. While it is said king Uzziah did what was right in the eyes of the Lord there is a huge malfunction in his leadership, *the high places were not taken away;* the people still sacrificed and burned incense (to other gods) on the high places. Uzziah also took liberties that were reserved for the priests only. He was reprimanded by a priest named Azariah and eighty (80) of his colleagues. The king became so angry at their supposed lack of respect that leprosy broke out immediately on his forehead. His neglect and disobedience are given as the reason for the king's being struck with leprosy.

What do we see in Uzziah's example:

- We need the root of our bondage to be broken
- We need to take down our high places
- We need any haughtiness or pride in our attitude to be destroyed

I don't know what your high place is but you do and it must be surrendered at the foot of the cross, otherwise it will lead you to sickness and death. God has to be able to trust you in a place of authority because once we get saved we become "heirs; heirs of God, and joint-heirs with Christ," **not** independently powerful.

God is a God of order and we must reverence His kingdom way. Ironically, the very meaning of Uzziah's name, "my strength is Yahweh," the king himself forgot. You will never be successful at anything you put your hands to do unless the Lord keeps you.

So, then it was *after* king Uzziah dies Isaiah was able to see the Lord. After we remove *our* high places that block our spiritual view *then* like Isaiah we can see the Lord in His proper place, sitting on a throne, high and lifted up. Your high place will hinder you from seeing His awesome majesty. We can shake the dust of our struggles under our feet when they are trampled by the hand of *the* Almighty God.

We're now prepared to handle the truth, **Isaiah 6:5, *"Then said I, Woe is me! I am undone; because I am a man of unclean lips, and I dwell in the midst of a people of unclean lips: for mine eyes have seen the King, the Lord of hosts."*** I am able to see the real me in true worship. I see my doom, my sinfulness, my wretchedness as well as those around me. Why? I have seen THE KING! The Lord of heaven's armies. Filthiness in the light of His holiness is magnified a trillion times over and this is the reason many people never come into relationship with Christ; they don't get through the process of worship.

Verses 6 & 7, *"Then flew one of the seraphims unto me, having a live coal in his hand, which he had taken with the tongs from off the altar: and he laid it upon my mouth, and said, Lo, this hath touched my lips; and thine iniquity is taken away, and thy sin is purged."* The minute some of us begin to move from Praise to Worship we abort that critical moment when Heaven gets their assignments to move on behalf of God for the sake of His people. One of the angels came from that same glory with a live coal from off the altar, the place of sacrifice and, understand this, true worship requires we conform to God's directives even as this angel did. In that place, the glory of God touched Isaiah; he was forgiven and purging there.

But wait that's not all, look at the outcome of this amazing time in the presence of God. **Isaiah 6:8** says, *"Also I heard the voice of the Lord, saying, 'Whom shall I send, and who will go for us?' Then said I, 'Here am I; send me."* Despite my offense to God, despite my lack of qualifications, and my questioning my readiness – He asks the question as I lay before Him, Oh bless His name. Once I'm in His glory and made anew, He only sees what He created me to be NOT what I was! Once you have a real experience with the true and living God, you will never be the same. And He takes us from glory to glory. My answer is send me, I'm all Yours!

If you've been fighting against your Throne Room Experience you are delaying your divine destiny. Believe God now! Begin to Worship now! Let His glory be revealed to you now! Your forgiveness is there, your deliverance is there, your freedom is there, your fruitfulness is there, your divine calling is there, your heavenly assignment is there. The all of who you are to be in Christ is there. *Get to the Throne of God...*

How Ya' Livin'?

In the days we're living in we should approach each day as an opportunity to serve the Lord Jesus; to bring Him glory and to lift up His name but in the words of a slang phrase, may I ask – How Ya' Livin'!?!

Is God going to be limited in what He reveals to us today because we have haven't *received* the truths we learned yesterday? Will He be able to show us His magnificence or will we simply settle for 'He woke me up this morning?'

One of the major truths permeating in my life: love and obedience are directly related. *Jesus said, **"If ye love me, keep my commandments."** He went on to say, **"If a person really loves me, he will keep my word (obey my teaching); and my Father will love him, and we will come to him and make our home (abode, special dwelling place) with him."** (TLB) This is so good. The Lord won't visit me every now and then. I won't happen up on His presence but He promised He will live with me / in me. He'll walk with me and talk with me and tell me I'm His own – if I obey Him because this lets Him know I really love Him. Not how emotional I am, or how well I serve in my respective place. *Jesus is asking us, will you show me your love by putting it into action?* The Lord wants to know – 'How Ya' Livin?'

Many of us have praised, worshipped, danced, cried and gotten off the floor while in the move of God only to leave that moment and almost immediately disobey His Word. He's holding us accountable to produce good fruit after His seeds of love are planted in us. Here are some scriptural mandates: **"Thou shalt love the Lord thy God with all thy heart, and with all thy soul, and with all thy mind. This is the first and great commandment."** So, why do we give God so little of ourselves, our time? (And I'm not talking about going to church.) Are you hungry for more of God? Do you thirst for His presence? Are you still anxious to hear what God is saying to you after the revival is over? *"And the second is like unto it, Thou shalt love thy neighbor as thyself."* God help us. Will we spend major time today avoiding our neighbor? Tolerating our neighbor? Or will we see our neighbor through the eyes of God. *"By this shall all men know that ye are my disciples, if ye have love one to another."* Not by how many people you claim got saved under your witness. Do men see us loving each other in the love of the Lord or are we still competing to see who performs the best? Are we reaching out in sincere compassion when a brother or sister is in distress? *"Beware of the scribes which love to go in long clothing, and love salutations in the marketplaces, and the chief seats in the synagogues, and the uppermost rooms at feasts..."* We love our places of prominence and seats of stature but if we were never 'seen' would we be found loving God by obeying Him? <u>Would we do the right thing just because we love Him that much?</u> 'How Ya' Livin?'

We could never repay God for all of His wonderful goodness to us but is your life of obedience telling the Lord you love Him? Are you stirring Him to draw closer from your scent of submission? *"For God so loved the world, that He gave His only begotten Son, that whosoever believeth in Him should not perish, but have everlasting life." "For I say unto you, that this that is written must yet be accomplished in me, And He was reckoned among the transgressors: for the things concerning me have an end." "Father, if thou be willing, remove this cup from me: nevertheless not my will but thine be done."* God the Father loved us so very much that He gave us Jesus, His only begotten Son. Jesus loved us so much that He knew He would be separated from His Father but He gave His life as the ultimate act of obedience. Now I ask you – do you love Him enough to obey? To deny yourself so that Christ may live in you?

This is the result of an obedient life in Jesus, *"As the Father hath loved me, so have I loved you: continue ye in my love. If ye keep my commandments, ye shall abide in my love; even as I have kept my Father's commandments, and abide in His love. These things have I spoken unto you, that my joy might remain in you, and that your joy might be full."* 'How Ya' Livin!?!'

*Every scripture used in the article is from the words of Jesus.

Dr. Charlene Nelson

HIS Goodness, My Reference

Has the Lord brought you through any storms lately? Has He sent healing? Has God worked any miracles with your name on it? Has He delivered you out of a situation that was designed to kill you? As a recipient of God's goodness and mercy there should be a never-ending praise going on in your spirit. But wait, there are even greater promises and rewards for those who genuinely want to experience relationship with God and not just material blessings.

Read our text carefully:

"Moses said to the Lord, See, You say to me, Bring up this people, but You have not let me know whom You will send with me. Yet You said, I know you by name and you have also found favor in My sight. Now therefore, I pray You, if I have found favor in Your sight, show me now Your way, that I may know you [to progressively become more deeply and intimately acquainted with You, perceiving and recognizing and understanding more strongly and clearly] *and that I may find favor in Your sight. And* [Lord, do] *consider that this nation is Your people. And the Lord said, My Presence shall go with you, and I will give you rest. And Moses said to the Lord, If Your Presence does not go with me; do not carry us up from here! For by what shall it be known that I and Your people have found favor in your sight? Is it not in Your going with us so that we are distinguished, I and Your people, from all the other people upon the face of the earth? And the Lord said to Moses, I will do this thing also that you have asked, for you have found favor, lovingkindness, and mercy in My sight and I know you personally and by name. And Moses said, I beseech You, show me Your glory. And God said, I will make all My goodness pass before you, and I will proclaim My name, THE LORD, before you; for I will be gracious to whom I will be gracious, and will*

show mercy and lovingkindness on who I will show mercy and lovingkindness." **Exodus 33:12-19** (The Amplified Bible)

For anyone who is born again the reality of salvation brings peace and joy. However, for those who believe to see the goodness of the Lord in the land of the living – salvation is not the end but rather a foundation; a foundation for a spiritually healthy and productive life in Christ. Moses spoke to God from the depths of his soul, such that I needed to translate his convictions with my own words. "I know You called me and I know I have Your unmerited favor *but* I need more. ***Show me You Lord***, teach me Your way, I've got to see Your Glory! Grant me the blessedness of getting close to You; I want to recognize and be familiar with Your voice, Your touch, Your move, Your way, Your heart. So strong and clear that nothing and no one can tell me/lead me otherwise. I just don't want your blessings; I want the assurance of living in Your presence. So much so that, if Your presence doesn't go with me don't move us from here. What will I refer to? If You don't go Lord, what security do I have? It's Your Hand being on us, Your presence being with us and Your Spirit being in us that makes us stand out from everyone else. Without you we are like any other people with any other god – helpless and hopeless! ***So Lord God hear my earnest plea, show me your Glory!"***

God's response makes my spirit leap for joy – ***My goodness is going before you and My name will be proclaimed before you.*** **His Goodness, my reference.** How do I know I'm gonna make it? His Goodness is my reference. How do I know this vision will come to pass? His name will be spoken on it and living in it before we even get there. Hallelujah to the Lamb of God!

From now on when the Lord shines His Goodness on your life (no matter how small) don't take it lightly. Consider that a moment to bless Him and ask for a greater enlightenment into the heart of God. How? By thanking Him, He knows you are acknowledging His power, goodness and mercy in every moment of favor towards you. A grateful heart is like a tender kiss in the heart of God. You are coming back to love Him for loving you like only HE can! Thus, Worship is born! You're open, you're ready, and you long to see His glory in every aspect of your life – what a wonderful gift that is to God. In my desire to accomplish Your perfect will for me – they must see that it's You, LORD. HIS Goodness, my reference. Give Him praise right now…

The BODY of CHRIST

"When you enter HIS Sanctuary, don't be limited to what's expected but rather come with a SPIRIT OF EXPECTANCY!"

CORPORATE GATHERINGS

Regarding Corporate Worship, (while it is a necessity to have in order to maintain a vibrant, productive church ministry), we must be sensitive to the reality that what we render publicly is still a very *private* expression. In an environment of sincere *Praise & Worship*, we bond as a collective body of Believers. Then what happens? Our collective hearts and spirits join to Jesus, our Blessed Savior. So, whether you are a pastor, minister, worship leader, etc., the people we worship with corporately must be able to find and settle into a place of security in our leadership. They may not know you personally but evidence of God's <u>real</u> anointing should allow them to trust the instruction, guidance and example you represent as the Lord's vessel. I say real anointing because there are those that give us a *facsimile* of the anointing, those who exploit man's emotions and keep us in the 'soulish' realm. Without compromise we've got to trust the God who made us to meet every need present during worship according to His perfect will. Therefore, our main objective is to present an atmosphere that welcomes the Lord's presence *thus* His glory. No service is based on man's abilities, we are inconsistent by nature but we can certainly depend on the faithfulness of our God.

As a member of the family of God, you must understand your responsibilities individually – whatever we are independently, we bring to the corporate setting. If you're inconsistent with your personal time with God, you can hinder the overall flow; if you're empty, you will leave a hole in that body of Believers; if you seek God daily, you will be a vital part of building the foundation for the manifested presence of God. **The corporate outcome is only a result of every individual input.** So, we must also make sure each person represented in the service is not getting lost in the masses. This does not mean we walk up to each person you feel is not showing enough emotion because we worship in spirit and in truth. So then, the question for us as individual Worshippers (in a corporate setting) is, *"If I were the only one giving God Praise, would He be pleased or would He have to look for another?"*

In many ways, the house of God has been desecrated to an 'Entertainment Capital' where performers practice to give their most outstanding display of talent and God is no where around. Meanwhile, the congregation (audience) often takes on the same mindset as those sitting in the Apollo Theater waiting to applaud or boo those who are on the stage. God help us! *Why are we wasting our time gathering if Jesus is not the primary reason?* How grieved He must be at our pretentious behavior. Lack of knowledge, ignorance, misplaced tradition or fear is no excuse for not honoring the King of kings. The Word of God is our key to truth. **Psalm 50:5 & 14** (The Amplified Bible) says, *"Gather together To Me My saints* **[those who have found grace in My sight]***, those who have made a covenant with Me by sacrifice. Offer to God the sacrifice of thanksgiving and pay your vows to the Most High."* Even the outright rebellious are warned about performing rituals that have no spiritual value. **Psalm 50:16-17** (TAB) says, *"But to the wicked, God says, What right have you to recite My statutes or take My covenant or pledge on your lips, seeing that you hate instruction and correction and cast My words behind you* [discarding them]*?"* We've got to search His Word in order to know His heart as to what will please the God of our salvation.

I must stress with great urgency here you must have *Worshipping Pastors*. The congregation must see the 'Head of the House' wholeheartedly involved and supporting this vital area in order to appreciate the major influence of praise and worship in the life of a victorious Believer. If the pastor comes in after Praise & Worship what message is that sending to the congregation? Or what if you're a ministry leader and you're always late for Praise and Worship, what message are you sending to the congregation? The message: Praise and Worship is not important, it's optional. As leaders we need to convey with great conviction nothing else in our services will flow right if we have not entered into the presence of God; that is where His anointing is released.

Those responsible for Praise & Worship within a local church must walk hand-in-hand with their Pastor(s) to establish an atmosphere that welcomes the Lord to take charge of each gathering. Praise & Worship gets stale, unsatisfactory and even boring when it is based on the limited abilities of a leader, however, when we lock into God we are stepping back and allowing the Holy Spirit to operate in its' full capacity. We have no idea of knowing what the needs of the people are but the Lord does and He guarantees to meet every one at the point of their need when given His total place of priority. Most importantly, the perfect plan of God will be revealed and set in motion. Remember, it is not about us but ALL about ***JESUS***!

We have come into this house
Gathered in His name to worship Him
Worship Him ~ Christ our Lord

So, forget about yourself and
Consecrate on Him and worship Him
Worship Him ~ Christ our Lord

Let us lift up holy hands
Magnify His name and worship Him
Worship Him ~ Christ our Lord

BUILD UP WHAT'S TORN DOWN

There are certain Godly characteristics that should be present when the body of Christ is gathered. We have allowed the enemy to pervade the significance of a united front. Sometimes Satan's best offense is to make us feel like we have to defend ourselves against each other. As long as the enemy can get us to fight each other, he knows we will be distracted and ineffective. *"The thief cometh not, but for to steal, and to kill, and to destroy..."* The devil wants to steal the refuge, strength and joy we get from the church; he wants to kill all of the blessings that God has for us before we can get them; and he wants to destroy the purpose of assembling ourselves together. But Jesus paid the price for another plan, *"...I am come that they might have life, and that they might have it more abundantly."* (**John 10:10**)

Remember, people of God, we are on the same side. Our relationships within the church should be representative of the love of God but very often they are more of an embarrassment to our Master. Relationships filled with misunderstanding, misconceptions, misjudgments, jealousy, competition, envy, lack of support, lack of respect, and the list goes on and on. If we claim to love the Lord as we do, the Bible offers us a convicting question, *"If a man says, I love God, and hateth his brother, he is a liar: for he that loveth not his brother whom he hath seen, how can he love God whom he hath not seen?"* (**I John 4:20**) This makes things absolutely clear. Jesus said in **Matthew 22:38-39**, *"That the first and great commandment is to love Him with all of our heart, soul and mind"* but He didn't stop there. Jesus said, *"And the second is like unto it, Thou shalt love thy neighbor as thyself."* Why are we struggling for position, coming against one another when NO flesh should glory in His presence? It's not about you and me, it's ALL about JESUS! The church in so many instances has assisted the enemy to the point that all he had to do was sit back and laugh. The thought of that ought to stir up our righteous indignation. We are grieving God! Just like it upsets a mother and father in the natural when their children are not getting along the same applies to our heavenly Father. We have the same Father, the same Daddy. He loves us all. We all have a place in His heart. There is enough of Him to go around without anyone being left out, overlooked or neglected. Can't you feel the Father's warmth and the glory of His smile when we are serving Him as loving, spiritual siblings? Each of us when operating under His redeeming grace and love are a dimension of the immeasurable magnitude of God. Let's not waste any more time fighting each other, we have to remove the mess before He can bless us. Whatever it takes we must come together, *"By this shall all men know that ye are my disciples, if ye have love one to another."* (**John 13:35**) The Bible says, *"If God be for us, who can be against us?"* (**Romans 8:31b**) This not only applies individually but corporately. How can He be for us when we're not about Him? The motive behind everything we do and say should be: God gets <u>ALL</u> the glory! *"That, according as it is written, he that glorieth, let him glory in the Lord."* (**Corinthians 1:31**)

With this in mind, believers must be aware of what our roles are as a family; more specifically as a Praise & Worship family. Our primary responsibilities are to lead the people of God to a united place of worship, as well as open the way for the Spirit to prepare us to receive His Holy Word. Pastors must be able to depend on worship leaders and trust them to assist whenever the need should arise. Our prayer is to always serve God in spirit and in truth. And remember, *"Who you are in Christ is far more important than what you do!"*

Worshipper's, let's get to the point where we can leave our individuality in order to link up with other Believers. The church is the bride of Christ and the bridegroom needs to feel at home with His family. There is a community (local, national and global) which looks to the foundation of gathered Believers for encouragement, strength, guidance and help. The Word reminds us one can chase a thousand but two can chase ten thousand. Sometimes there are certain advantages that are only offered to a group. For instance, when you go to some of these dining places, they have specials that are meant to inspire a larger purchase, which in essence says, the more of you there is the better. Where there is unity, there is strength! *"Endeavouring to keep the unity of the Spirit in the bond of peace. There is one body, and one Spirit..."*

As a Worshipping Body we have 3 central areas which must be in operation:

1. **Know together** – Know who Jesus is and what your collective purpose is in Him. Understand the need(s) the Holy Spirit has assigned for you to meet as a unit.

2. **Grow together** – Everybody is somebody in Christ, there is no big I and little you. Follow your leader's plan according to the leading of the Lord. Fulfill the divine destiny placed before you.

3. **Sow together** – If you sow Godly things together then you will reap Godly benefits. True laborers can expect an abundant harvest.

THANK YOU LORD FOR REMEMBERING US

Although most sincere Believers do all they can to live according to God's Word, we still find ourselves down and out sometimes. This is especially hard to accept when you've just come from the mountaintop, i.e., a rich service, a stirring prayer meeting, an eye-opening Bible study, an unforgettable time in praise & worship, a power-packed revival or a life-changing moment. When the glory lifts, you are in the valley. How did I get here? But more than that, how did I get here *so soon*? I felt so close to God but now He and the answers to my prayer seem so far away. Fear not my friend, be encouraged. The Lord wants you to hear His Word. **Psalm 136:23-24** says, *"Who remembered us in our low estate: for His mercy endureth for ever: And hath redeemed us from our enemies: for His mercy endureth for ever."* The devil would love for you to believe God has forgotten all about you; to think you're going to stay down and never get back up but the devil is a liar. **The Lord remembers us in our low estate**. You may be hurting now, you have just come from a painful time or you may have to go through something soon but wherever you are don't forget, **the Lord remembers us in our low estate.**

There are three types of lows: 1) **Self-induced lows**; 2) **Enemy-influenced lows**; and 3) **Ordained lows**. Whichever one should arise in your life, position yourself in the Word so that 'Low' will not overtake you. We are not only fighting for our lives but for the *manifestation of God's glory*. *"Thy will be done on earth, as it is in heaven."* I heard Gloria Copeland say something that was simple but yet quite profound, "Jesus has all power over Satan and left him with nothing but a mouth." I've learned to realize it's a mouth that lies to us as much as he can trying to make us question our Almighty God and too many times he's very convincing. But he would have less and less access to our spirit if we would feed ourselves *constantly* on the Word. Whether we are at fault or have been chosen to suffer for the sake of Christ, there is not a situation we can experience that is not covered in the scriptures. Find strength in the Word. Find Hope. Find Correction. Find Mercy and Grace. Find Forgiveness. Find Answers. Find Direction. Find Peace. Find the Lord and look up. ***We praise you God and thank you Lord for remembering us in our low estate.***

GET READY TO BE A BLESSING

Announcement to the body of Christ: <u>We must be in a constant state of preparedness</u>. Our scriptural basis for this mandate is **Philippians 1:20-21**, *"According to my earnest expectation and my hope, that in nothing I shall be ashamed, but that with all boldness, as always, so now also Christ shall be magnified in my body, whether it be by life, or by death. For to me to live is Christ, and to die is gain."*

God does not empower us for the purpose of being showcased in the four walls of our churches. The world is in desperate need of a spiritual outpouring and our answer is in **Matthew 6:10**, *"Thy kingdom come. Thy will be done in earth, as it is in heaven."* (The emphasis of this verse cannot be overstated.) Once we have the 'Victor' living inside us, we prepare ourselves as submitted disciples, who are fixed and effective. We can't afford to lose anymore valuable time.

I went through an unbelievable situation where people who were extremely disobedient and harmful seem to be elevated even though the leadership was well aware of their actions. I was outraged that major issues and the need for anointing were being ignored and everything was being presented as 'right and good.' Then one night, while sitting in my car, I heard the Lord say very softly to me, *"I CAN'T USE YOU LIKE THIS…"* I felt an even greater pain in my heart. I said, "Like what?" The Lord kept talking, *"You're getting hard, and you're beginning to get bitter. You are taking it personally because you know there are some who are standing in position that are far from me and you so desire for the world to experience My glory."* The Lord was helping me identify my pain. Then the Holy Spirit filled my car and the Lord said, *"Let it go, tell me all…Come unto me, Charlene. You have labored and you are heavy laden but I <u>will</u> give you rest. Take my yoke upon you, and learn of me, I'm meek and lowly in heart. You need* *rest for your soul. My yoke is easy and my burden is light."* I cried and cried, yelled and cried some more, then I honestly (without fear) shared my anger, hurt and overwhelming sadness to the Lord. When I calmed down, The Comforter engulfed me and held me. The Lord forgave me and set me free from those things that were not like Him and said these words, *"You love me, you learn of me and I <u>will</u> give you rest."* For the first time in months, I slept peacefully.

The Lord told me to share this with you because many times we are held up by our own inability to release things to the hand of God. The enemy was sapping my strength every moment I relived the injustice being done. During that period, I was more focused on man than I was on God. I had to trust that God in His own way and own time would bring deliverance and He did – when I let Him be God, *not* me. The lesson is to stay focused on God, His purpose, His plan and His promises. He sees and knows all things. His ways are not our ways; His thoughts are not our thoughts and be assured He does all things well. So, never let the devil waltz you out of your place in the kingdom. *Be ready at all times*. You are blessed to be a blessing. *"And not only so, but we glory in tribulations also: knowing that tribulation worketh patience; and patience, experience; and experience, hope: and hope maketh not ashamed; <u>because the love of God is shed abroad in our hearts by the Holy Ghost which is given to us</u>."*

GOD'S GUIDELINES FOR PREPAREDNESS

A. **The In-Heart Agenda**. "Jesus said unto him, Thou shalt love the Lord thy God with all thy heart, and with all thy soul, and with all thy mind." **(Matthew 22:37)**

B. **The In-Service Agenda**. "If anyone serves Me, he must continue to follow Me [to cleave steadfastly to Me, conform wholly to My example in living and, if need be, in dying] and wherever I am, there will My servant be also, if anyone serves Me, the Father will honor Him." **(John 12:26** / TAB)

C. **The In-House Agenda**. "Through wisdom is an house builded; and by understanding it is established: and by knowledge shall the chambers be filled with all precious and pleasant riches." **(Proverbs 24:3-4)**

D. **The In-Public Agenda**. "Even as the Son of man came not to be ministered unto, but to minister, and to give His life a ransom for many." **(Matthew 20:28)**

Let's be prepared. Let's be ready, the world needs to know the Blessed Savior!

Words to prepare you for the 2nd half of

PRAISENTATIONS

The times we're living in calls for the people of God to offer unto Him real praise & true Worship. Many of us are simply not exposed to Praise & Worship services which truly give glory, honor and majesty to God. In this day of religious tradition when people are still praising and worshipping God in the same old form and fashion, and often, without true conviction, I'm so glad God has raised up a holy, spirit-filled pastor, worship leader, a daughter of Judah (that tribe of Israel sent out first into battle with the praises of God) who is not afraid to sound the alarm of Praise intended to tear down Satan's walls of sin and break the chains of spiritual despair.

I am not a worship leader nor am I a praise team member. In fact, until I witnessed the ministry of *Charlene Nelson* the only thing I knew about Praise & Worship was it took up a half hour on Sunday morning with old hymns and testimonies. Not until I experienced the move of God in this divinely-inspired liturgy of Praise & Worship did I know the power it held to change my spiritual life from near complete darkness to sublime light. Not until I experienced the outpouring of God's spirit did I learn to worship God in spirit and truth. Under this ministry my spirit was reawakened and today, I gladly practice Praise & Worship principles in my daily walk with Christ.

The ministry of *Charlene Nelson* has exhorted, blessed, healed and delivered <u>as God has used His chosen vessel</u> to minister unto countless members of the body of Christ. It is with great pleasure and sincere honor I recommend this book (<u>in totality</u>) for your reading enjoyment and edification. As you apply these spiritual principles, you will experience a transformation in your life. You will be moved out of spiritual stagnation into glorious restoration. You will see how praise will open doors to a closer walk with God and worship will lead to a more personal relationship with Him. Praise & Worship is essential to your spiritual growth and consecration. So, let this book urge you to discover new dimensions.

In joy...Tracy Fuller – New York, NY

The DEEP CALLETH unto the DEEP

"Ask for an ANOINTING to <u>LIVE THIS DAY</u>
not just to perform a task!"

The DEEP CALLETH unto the DEEP

(Everybody must understand the function of Worship Leaders)

This section is to encourage, uplift and inspire those of us who have been chosen to lead God's people through Praise & Worship. Words of refreshing for your spirit as you seek God continually – so you can take others to Him. It also serves to give others insight to the Worship Leaders responsibility to God and the body of Christ, allowing us to pray more effectively for those in this sacred office.

A SACRED TRUST

To lead Praise & Worship is a **SACRED** Trust:

Study (*scripture and song*) so we may

Answer the divine call to lead with an humble

Confidence in order to make

Ready the hearts and minds of

Every Believer to

Do that which is pleasing to God!

By God's directives we're developing environments where human abilities end and the Holy Ghost begins. In other words, when we've done all that's within our capability in accordance to His Word, we can be assured God's power will be made manifest!

SEVEN FRUITS OF NECESSITY

For Building a Powerful Praise & Worship Team Ministry: *Appointing a Dedicated Leader*

These seven fruits of necessity seem simple but are true staples for trustworthy men and women to lead us to the throne.

1. Saved with a genuine love and reverence for the Lord

2. Faithful/committed to your local church

3. Consistent in tithes & offerings

4. Love, respect and cherish your pastor(s). Work directly under the pastor's authority and vision.

5. Spiritually balanced (through proven vehicles - Bible Study, personal worship, enjoying the fellowship of Godly relationships, a peaceful home base, etc.)

6. Establishing and maintaining a strong kinship and work bond with the Praise Team. The Worship Leader should have a clear understanding of the purpose for which this ministry exists

7. Gifted in song. Able to develop a scripture-based repertoire which includes a wide variation of song styles, Ephesians 5:19 and Colossians 3:16. Able to effectively induce corporate Praise & Worship as the Holy Spirit directs

Special Note: Along with this critical guideline, we must mention to separate yourself from worldly influences that could infiltrate your spirit thus taking away quality areas where only God should have access. This is where discipline and consecration determine the overall success of your Praise & Worship ministry.

Many people (including those who lead us) have misconceptions about the 'Worship Leader' they are now considered the deep ones; the ones that were born to sing and live to sing but *if you're not in love with Christ your song will never live or give life*!

MY TOW TRUCK THEORY

I was riding along one day and saw an unusual sight – a tow truck being towed. At first I chuckled but then something was ignited in my spirit. Tow trucks were invented with the purpose of helping disabled or stalled vehicles. In addition to taking vehicles to a place where they can be serviced, they also give jump starts or do on-the-spot repairs if the problem is not too complex. *Imagine the helper needing help.*

I was reminded of Moses and the Israelites when they were at war with the Amalekites in Exodus. *"But the warriors of Amalek came to fight against the people of Israel at Rephidim. Moses instructed Joshua to issue a call to arms to the Israelites, to fight the army of Amalek. "Tomorrow," Moses told him, "I will stand at the top of the hill, with the rod of God in my hand!" So Joshua and his men went out to fight the army of Amalek. Meanwhile Moses, Aaron, and Hur went to the top of the hill. And as long as Moses held up the rod in his hands, Israel was winning; but whenever he rested his arms at his sides, the soldiers of Amalek were winning. Moses' arm finally became too tired to hold up the rod any longer; so Aaron and Hur rolled a stone for him to sit on, and they stood on each side, holding up his hands until sunset. As a result, Joshua and his troops crushed the army of Amalek, putting them to the sword."* (**Exodus 17:8-13**)

Moses was the living vessel through which deliverance came to the people of Israel. He was without a doubt God's choice to lead His people. However, at this juncture, as Moses stood before the people for divine inspiration he did something very human, he grew weary. One of the hardest things for any good leader to admit at times is we get weary. Yes, you're giving God and His people everything you have. Yes, you have prepared and are ready to stand before God's army singing, praising and shouting exhortations that provide strength but sometimes we get too tired. As we embark to serve God daily we must learn what to do when we get weary. This passage of scripture tells us what to do. **Surround yourself with trustworthy armorbearers**.

Aaron and Hur did three things that every spirit-filled armorbearer should know.

The first thing: Aaron and Hur rolled a stone for Moses to sit on.

Your armorbearer must provide a place for you to rest. How? Intercessory prayer. A comforting Word. An attentive ear. Leading *you* into worship. Just to name a few. They like Aaron and Hur were there to help before the battle was lost, your armorbearer should be there to help you *before* you faint or fall from weariness.

The second thing: Aaron and Hur stood by Moses' side.

They were a wall of support. The bared him up when Moses got weary, they were there for Moses to lean on. They didn't approach Moses harshly demanding to know what his problem was. They recognized his weariness *before* it could overtake him, which would result in the Israelites losing the battle. What's significant here is there was more at stake than just Moses' life. The Amalekites were trying to destroy the Israelites, God's nation, God's people, God's leader. When you get tired there's more at stake than just you. You lead God's people and whether you know it or not they look to you to help lead them to victory. That's why the enemy fights you so very hard. If he can get you to stop blessing God, he knows the people you lead will be affected by that. It doesn't matter whether those same people ever stop to acknowledge the sacrifice you make as the Worship Leader or whether they accuse you of doing a half done job.

Many times after their exit from Egypt the Israelites told Moses he led them away only for them to die but when it came time to get an answer from God who did they look to? Moses.

And lastly, Aaron and Hur held up Moses' hands for him.

You need an armorbearer that will do whatever it takes to make sure you stay in the right position. Moses' assistants could have approached his weariness the wrong way. They could have said, "This doesn't make any sense how tired he is, the people don't appreciate him anyway. Let's put him to bed and let him get some rest." Do you have armorbearers that are so busy protecting you they are not seeing the overall purpose of God in each situation? There are times when love and concern can be misguided. You need armorbearers that know what's best for the state you're in; *armorbearers that work with the plan of God and not against it.*

Don't be afraid to admit you're too tired but make sure you have a good tow truck. If He has not already, I pray God will send you the armorbearer that best suits the need in your life according to God's plan.

LOOK IN, LINE UP, LET LOOSE:
OUR PROCESS OF RENEWAL

With everything going on in the world more and more people are being drawn to the church and some resemblance of peace. Whether they are drawn out of *desperation, fear, weariness* or just plain *curiosity*, it is our responsibility as the Worship Leader to create an atmosphere that welcomes the pure presence of God. But often times the same conditions people are drawn by are the same conditions we attempt to lead worship by. *Desperately* going through the motions of the Praise & Worship service but knowing God is not there. *Fearful* of experiencing yet another Sunday of failure and disappointment. *Weary* so much so you're drained before you even start. *Curiosity* leads you rather than the Holy Spirit. You think things like, "I wonder if I did it this way would the people respond differently?"

STOP!!! SHAKE YOURSELF → WAKE UP → DON'T GO ANY FURTHER UNTIL YOU TAKE HEED TO THESE WORDS!

As Worship Leaders, our daily spiritual upkeep is essential to our corporate settings. We must **LOOK IN, LINE UP** and **LET LOOSE**. Before you can select a song, prepare for rehearsal, meet with your Team or anything else, you've got to <u>*go to God daily for yourself*</u>.

    A. <u>**LOOK IN**</u>. *"Create in me a clean heart, O God; and renew a right spirit within me."* (**Psalm 51:11**) Ask the Lord to turn the search light on and keep it on. Place those shortcomings, insecurities, inadequacies and sins on the altar of God. If we're going to present fresh dew from Heaven (not just a new song) in our Worship services, there has to be constant opportunities for God to work *in* us (and *on* us), so He can work *through* us. Don't get so bogged down with the duties of leading worship that God has to work around you and not through you.

B. **LINE UP**. *"Saying, Father, if thou be willing, remove this cup from me: nevertheless not my will, but thine be done."* (**Luke 22:42**) Most Worship Leaders, if asked, will tell you they prefer not want to lead worship. Like Jesus, they have asked at one time or another, the cup be removed. Remember, the devil has a special hate for those of us who now lead others to the throne of God so he attacks us with intense, almost unending persecution and tribulation. But what's most important to note here is the devil is already defeated. So, then forget everything the enemy has used to discourage or demoralize us. We must even forget our own plans and align ourselves with the perfect will of God. Anything less is a compromise which offends the Lord. Go forth no matter what the cost. Let it be God's way or no way.

C. **LET LOOSE**. *"He that believeth on me, as the scripture hath said, out of his belly shall flow rivers of living water."* (**John 7:38**) The moment you understand it is your confidence in Christ (He that believeth on me – [**Jesus**]) not yourself that makes you able, then you will experience the rivers of living water coming out of *your* belly to bless God's people. Trust the God in you, don't limit Him to what your frail humanity can produce. Expect the supernatural power of God to guide you (and those you minister with/to) from glory to glory. Living Waters. Waters that give life. Waters that sustain true life. Waters that keep you healthy and alive. Waters that will heal and refresh someone else's life. Let Loose, Let Go, Let God!

Hold on to this **Process of Renewal**. Come back to it when you need it. Allow it to become a part of your daily walk with Christ. You will see a beautiful transformation in your spirit, in your life and in your ministry. To God be the glory for the things He is going to do…

"I'LL TAKE YOU THERE"

The Worship Leaders Decree

Does leading worship ever get any easier? Do I have to be on this rollercoaster ride every week? Is there any refuge in familiarity? Why do they look at me like that? Will they like this new song? Why can't I get the Praise Team to understand the difference between concert performance and corporate participation?

And the questions go on and on with new ones being added every service. While I sense in my spirit God's delight in the church renewing their vows to Praise & Worship Him (both privately and publicly), I also sense God's frustration in us as Worship Leaders due to our inability to effectively lead His people to the throne with any type of consistency. Either we experience the 'hit or miss' method or we become settled in on the 'sure fired, they love this song list.

We must operate in the authority of Christ if we are going to have an impact as a leader on those we lead. Oh, it's not easy, I know but God has carefully mapped out instructions for us to follow. *Those instructions are found in His Word*, (which is more like a treasure map, you find endless riches the more you stay in it). When you are a leader the spirit which you lead with is the spirit those you are leading take on. If you're unlearned in your role as a worshipper, the Praise Team and congregation will remain clueless. If you lead with a puffed-up, arrogant spirit, people will display their own offensive spirit(s) and freely I might add. If you cherish your relationship with God and seek Him diligently, people will want what they experience through your walk and desire to surrender their lives to the Lord. It's all in how you live. Your delivery in service is only a result of your day-to-day with Christ. (Those "off" days will be a rare exception.)

So how do we lead? As a worshipper how do I begin to reposition myself to stand in the gap for those I'm taking to His throne?

1. **Deuteronomy 32:12, "*So the Lord alone did lead him, and there was no strange god with him.*"** BE LED BY THE LORD! We are often guilty of studying other Worship Leaders (*first*) rather than adopting the life of Christ as our ultimate pattern. *We need to hear from God.* There is a distinct spiritual design He has created for you to work in. *Never value the example of others more than the example of Christ.* When Christ is truly the Head of your life as a Worship Leader this Word says no strange gods will show up. No spirit that will offend our God. Nothing that will shame His name. People will know we are serving (and leading them to) a true and living God.

2. **Luke 6:39, "*And He spake a parable unto them, Can the blind lead the blind? Shall they not both fall into the ditch?*"** RECEIVE SPIRITUAL AND PRACTICAL KNOWLEDGE! Study, instruction and training are essential. How can you take someone where you have not been? You mean you haven't been in God's presence all week and then you expect the people to respond to a request you don't honor yourself. We were all pretty emotional today but did we touch God? Your understanding of Praise & Worship is limited to whether you feel they responded with visible/audible evidence!?! Some of the most tremendous moves of God are in the stillness of His presence and you want the saints jumping, screaming and running-all the time! Study God's Word,

receive instruction through the Word and trustworthy teachers who believe the Word of God fully, not just the parts that fit their opinion, upbringing or worship-style. Get proper training through books, workshops/seminars, one-on-one sessions, etc. Be open to learn so you won't mislead the people you are responsible for.

3. **Jeremiah 31:9** (a&b / TLB), *"Tears of joy shall stream down their faces, and I will lead them home with great care. They shall walk beside the quiet streams and not stumble."* <u>LEAD WITH THE CONCERN OF A PARENT</u>! When you are in a loving environment you feel safe, guarded and protected. You can express yourself and grow. You can make mistakes without feeling threatened to be cut off or embarrassed. Worship Leaders we should serve with the spirit of a concerned parent. With great care to the spiritual welfare of all worshippers' within our fold. Leading with a humble assurance so those under our care will not stumble. There is nothing worse than being in worship service and being uncomfortable because the leader is unlearned, anxious, harsh, abrasive and accusatory. We can't afford to be selfish, for that moment of time we have been entrusted to take them to the Father. The One that heals all wounds, looks for every lost soul, turns mourning into dancing, answers all our terrifying questions with the warmth of His love. For that time we are in leadership of the people of God we serve as surrogate parents – we should be God in the flesh; surrendering our humanity to His total deity.

The next time you lay before God seeking His direction in leading His people, see the congregation you've been assigned to in your mind and say to them, "You can trust the God in me, I'll Take You There…"

*Special Note: This is one of the most insightful teachings the Lord has ever shared with me. I highly recommend this study to everyone and anyone who is responsible for holding rehearsals on a regular basis. Worship Leaders, Choir Directors/Presidents, Music Directors, Drama Instructors, Dance Teams, etc. No matter what differences in the particular settings, these jewels that will enrich your rehearsals exponentially.

THE INTIMACY OF REHEARSAL

There are many who are responsible for holding rehearsals to ensure a spirit of excellence while rendering service to the Lord first and then to our respective churches and ministries. However, many of us, if we'd be honest, dread rehearsals. Why? The pressure of staying prepared. The agony of presenting a new idea, concept or song. The heaviness of keeping the group you're leading interested for an hour or more – just to list a few concerns. Be encouraged my friend. We've all been there or are there. Our title seems to be a paradox but it is revelation waiting to be applied. Rest your spirit for a moment as I share with you some of the ways the Lord released me from the "heebee-geebee's" that come up when I'm getting ready for rehearsal.

Webster's Dictionary definitions:

Intimacy – most private/personal; close or familiar; deep/thorough

Rehearsal – to repeat, recount, practice for public performance

Webster's definitions are true in more ways than I care to admit. Many rehearsal settings have just become another playground for the enemy, rather than productive environments. We have seen rehearsals used as a pick-up spot, a gossip gathering, a competitive contest, a complaining campaign and simply where many of our group leaders discover their weaknesses and insecurities but we must reclaim our rehearsals for the purposes of Christ. Pray the Word of God with me right now, *"We bind every spirit that would seek to exalt itself against the knowledge of God and we bring into captivity every thought to the obedience of Christ. We loose real Praise and true Worship so that the Lord may be our Instructor as we seek to bring others into His glory. In Jesus name we pray, amen."*

As I open up certain aspects of things we look to accomplish in our rehearsals, see where your group is, what you may already be doing and what needs to be implemented.

1. The Presence of God should be the overwhelming factor in each and every rehearsal. *"For where two or more are gathered together in my name, there am I in the midst of them."* (**Matthew 18:20**) Don't be concerned about who is not there but work with who *is* there, (Jesus knew not to say where twenty or thirty). It will hinder your growth if you base your preparation on the most skilled members of the group. God has a way of perfecting the faithful in His presence. Teach your members to reverence the presence of God. I remember when we first got started I decided I would write a list of what we sang and who was there – the Lord rebuked me immediately. He said, "I want you to depend on me not in people; depend on my glory and not on a song – I will see you through." I've done that and He has always manifested Himself as we stand before His people. His Presence is primary.

2. Make sure no division is among you, that each member is treated as family. *"Now I beseech you, brethren, by the name of our Lord Jesus Christ, that ye all speak the same thing, and that there be no divisions among you; but that ye be perfectly joined together in the same mind and in the same judgment."* (**I Corinthians 1:10**) *"Behold, how good and how pleasant it is for brethren to dwell together in unity."* (**Psalms 133:1**) Both of these scriptures emphasize Family. You have a greater love, appreciation and tolerance for people when they are your family. As the saying goes, you can pick your friends

but not your family. If you have been a leader for any amount of time there has been or is someone assigned to your group and you wonder why in the world is the person here? They may be desperately in need of family and your group may be the way God decides to provide that for them. Hard to get along with? Yes! Always difficult and uncooperative? Yes! Less gifted than some of the others? Yes – but they're your brother or sister and God has entrusted them to your care. How good and how pleasant when the family of God dwells together on one accord. If your rehearsals are tense and tight; if you and your members feel like you're walking on eggshells because there's a section or member of the group that is so easily offended; if you continue to get phone calls after rehearsal about everything that was wrong at rehearsal, your group is not in unity. The best way to expose the enemy is to have open, honest, spirit-filled conversations while the group is together. The devil uses trivial things to bring division such as what color stockings, tie or no tie, do the verse one or twice – no division. Whether your members are there for a season or there until the Lord returns consider them your family and your approach to leadership will be a blessing to them and bring honor to Christ.

3. Make sure your members have a strong work ethic and regard your rehearsals as a place of safety and refuge. *"In the fear of the Lord is strong confidence: and His children shall have a place of refuge."* (**Proverbs 14:26**) Your members must reverence the Lord and put their trust in Him not in their abilities. Make sure they are not approaching the rehearsal with a 'too' casual, this is not the real thing' attitude. *If God never shows up in your rehearsal, it will be almost impossible to present Him in the*

actual service. Make sure you are not so rigid in your time with the group that the Lord is not able to change your agenda. He desires to be in the midst – even in rehearsal. Remember, we are family and they should not think about the upcoming rehearsal with disdain. A place of refuge – a retreat. Rehearsals should be refreshing, enjoyed, anticipated and challenging, both spiritually and in the area of their gifts. No one should be embarrassed because of a mistake but corrected with a firm, attentive hand. Do your members feel safe in your rehearsals?

4. Don't raise entertainers, Impart a Spirit of Praise & Worship. ***"And let the peace of God rule in your hears, to the which also ye are called in one body; and be ye thankful. Let the word of Christ dwell in you richly in all wisdom; teaching and admonishing one another in psalms and hymns and spiritual songs, singing with grace in your hearts to the Lord. And whatsoever ye do in word or deed, do all in the name of the Lord Jesus, giving thanks to God and the Father by Him."*** **(Colossians 3:15-17)** The reason some of us can not release a spirit of Praise & Worship throughout our congregation is because it has not been released in our groups. We have allowed the rehearsals to be so mechanical God is never invited in an intimate way to stir our hearts collectively closer to Him. This scripture says we have to teach, becoming a leader automatically requires you be a teacher. You don't have to know everything but as you seek God He will guide you and send you the help you need to lead with wisdom, anointing and practically. Don't be afraid or too proud to ask for help, there are probably members of your group who are skilled in areas you are not, waiting to be asked to assist and lighten your

load. We're serving to the glory of God. We're not in the star-making business. *Jesus is the only Star*! What good are we if we get all the notes right, know all the right movements, say all the right things but yet these all these things are not coming out of an aggregation of peaceful, thankful hearts. We don't want our efforts to be in vain. We must study and know His Word to know what God wants from us; God is looking to us to teach others.

5. Don't belittle the power of prayer. **"Even them will I bring to my holy mountain, and make them joyful in my house of prayer: their burnt offerings and their sacrifices shall be accepted upon mine altar; for mine house shall be called an house of prayer for all people."** (**Isaiah 56:7**) Some of us have made our corporate prayer time nothing more than a mechanical segment of our rehearsals. We need prayer; prayers that reach Heaven and get results; prayers that set the atmosphere; prayers that bring our hearts, minds and gifts into one accord. Prayer not only allows us to speak to God but He can direct us in that precious time. I also believe in having periodic prayer meetings for the Team which strengthens and renews focus / purpose. Personally, I don't feel a "prayer chaplain" is advantageous because each member will grow and seek God if they are asked to partake in the spiritual aspects of the ministry. I'm amazed at how many Believers feel uncomfortable if they have to pray publicly (which usually means they're not praying privately). Prayer opens the door to the intimacy I'm speaking of. It is not a choice but a necessity.

6. Know the songs you're presenting as if you wrote it. **"Who can understand his errors?"** (**Psalms 19:12a**) There is nothing worse than sitting in a rehearsal with a leader/teacher that is really not familiar with the

material and not prepared. It's an offense to those you are serving. It says what you all are doing was not/is not important enough for you to take quality time with it before you give it to us. *This discourages your group members greatly.* Moreover, the spirit of slothfulness, laziness or incompetence transfer to the Team/Group and it will show up when you stand before God and His people. As a result, the ministry may become stagnant and stagnation ruins anticipation. Expectancy should be the norm in your gatherings. If you have the gift to do what's required in the actual delivery of the ministry but not the ability to teach – you MUST have a partnership with a member that does. That means you and your teaching partner have to study the materials together prior to your rehearsal and come ready with order and a flow so there will be no embarrassing, unproductive stretches. The quickest way to get members to not come to rehearsal is to come unprepared. Live with the song. *Learn to love it even if you don't like it.* We have sung many songs that were not within my personal taste but they were aligned with the Word and the move of God for our house of worship; don't let preferences get in the way. In addition, on this point do not be one who changes the song every time you come back to teach it, this will breed confusion and lack of focus. Be creative but within reason and collective understanding.

7. Teach the group to share in the responsibility of productive time together. ***"But now are they many members, yet one body."*** (**I Corinthians 12:20**) Be prayerful and let the Holy Spirit reveal the member's strengths to you. *Put them to work*. If a member has the gift of intercession, let them know you need them to lift the group up before the Lord continually. If a member has the gift of

organization, let them handle the administrative end of things. People feel better about what they're doing when they can contribute to its success. Don't get burned out trying to be all things for all people – you're a family and you should operate as such.

8. Don't function under pressure but under Praise. *"The Lord will perfect that which concerneth me: thy mercy, O Lord, endureth forever: forsake not the works of Thine own hands."* (**Psalms 138:8**) Ministry should be a joy and not a burden and the joy of the Lord is your strength. If you're always run down, discouraged and defeated, it's not the Lord doing the work. Every God-ordained ministry is the work of God and He does not want us serving in our own might. Not by might, nor by power, but by My Spirit, says the Lord. Present your concerns to the One who does all things well – He will finish what He started.

I pray you will apply these Godly instructions to build up your area of ministry in the private times. There is a spiritual intimacy that should be in each one of our rehearsals. Remember to give time for bonding, testimonies, praise reports, prayer requests, member concerns and lots of hugs. May your rehearsals always be intimate.

Most sincerely…your sister in Christ.

THE CONTINUED LESSON

"And the things that thou hast heard of me among many witnesses, the same commit thou to faithful men, who shall be able to teach others also."

"And the instructions which ye have heard from me along with many witnesses, transmit and entrust (as a deposit) to reliable and faithful men who will be competent and qualified to teach others also." **(II Timothy 2:2** / TLB)

There is no question the number one priority for the body of Christ in the past several decades has been to get back to the place of Praise & Worship. Every denomination has realized how removed we were from the Word of God by not fulfilling His command to bless Him at all times and let His Praise be continually in our mouths. To understand God is a Spirit and they that worship Him must worship Him in spirit and in truth. My heart leaps with excitement as I go across this country experiencing God's people cry out for forgiveness and reach out for understanding in an area that is so sacred to the Lord Himself. I feel God even as I'm writing this, bless you Jesus.

Our subject is: THE CONTINUED LESSON. Jesus said in **John 8:31-32,** *"If ye continue in my word, then are ye my disciples indeed; And ye shall know the truth and the truth shall make you free."* So Praise & Worship Family, we must continue to search the Word of the Lord, seeking truth which will release freedom. All of our churches could stand more liberty in the Spirit. None of us are there. Our focus is to *know* the Word, so we can *be in* the Word, *operating by* the Word, *so we can experience the results through our practice of the Word.*

Paul said as you are instructed, advised, charged, introduced, settled in teachings of the Word (in this context as it pertains to a life of Praise & Worship) pass it on to someone else. Get a flow going. Let there be a progressive sequence of knowledge going throughout your Praise & Worship crew. Don't just share the latest new song but share your insights on God's desire for a worshipping body (remember everything must be based on the Word not our personal opinions). Paul also said teach reliable and faithful men who will be competent and qualified to teach others. Someone who knows the TV schedule better than they know where Lucifer's demise is in the Word is not qualified. Someone who knows who's dating in the church more readily than they know where to find Psalmists as they appear in the Word is not competent. You know who I'm talking about. Their major concern is not God's agenda so we have to be careful not to waste valuable time with the wrong people but for those who know we can't just sing but we must sing with understanding also, pour into them. Open the floodgates, share your soul. You will bless them.

Here are three simple but certain ways to keep THE CONTINUED LESSON going:

INVITE them to share the things of God with you. (The Word, Prayer, Worship & Praise and Wholesome Fellowship)

INVEST in their spirit. Impart that which you've been enlightened with. Your release of spiritual knowledge will help furnish them with power and authority to do what God is calling us to do.

INVOKE them to assist you in getting to the place of the blessing. To not use ignorance, fear, laziness or disobedience as an excuse from going higher in God.

The world says, "And the beat goes on." **Believers say, "My Praise shall be continually of thee."** May the LESSON CONTINUE...

YOU *ARE* WORKING FOR THE LORD

(*AREN'T* YOU)!?!

Recently, I had the privilege of speaking to a young lady who is approaching her final year of college. She desired to know whether she was moving in the direction God wanted her to go, doing the things God wanted her to do. (How refreshing that was to hear.) During the conversation I asked her where she worked. She said, "IHOP." (You know, International House of Pancakes.) And there was a slight pause. I said, "Well, you know there are things I apply to life daily that I learned in the secular workplace, although the job seemed to be insignificant at the time. She said, "It's funny you said that because right now I'm learning how to take orders from God and do them exactly like He asked!" Wow! That immediately grabbed my spirit! There are people leading others who have not learned this principle – we need God to help us.

In my travels, there have been many who have come up to me and told me how they so desire to be in full-time ministry. Yes, some of these individuals are being prepared for this but not everyone in fact not most. Full-time ministry is not the end all of Christian service. That's a serious misconception. Those of us who are in full-time ministry are not in a holding pattern, a euphoric state waiting for the Lord's return, we, just like all Believers have to strive to please God daily. The difference being sometimes the demonic attack(s) toward us is a lot more intense because we're responsible on a regular basis for feeding many other lives. I also want to point out here many who are now working full-time in the vineyard have put in years and years of dedicated labor in the world. And furthermore, everyone who is working full-time in religious matters is not about Jesus. There are those who simply have a job and not a ministry. So, now that that is clear, wherever you are employed, whatever kind of work you do, I ask you again, "You *ARE* working for the LORD (*AREN'T* you)!?!

Any true born again Believer knows the workplace is one of our greatest battlefields but it's also meant to: 1) provide income for us to get the natural things we need; 2) reach the lost; 3) establish discipline/principles in our walk with God and, 4) allow the light of the Lord to shine. Notice I did not put reach the lost first. Why? Because your secular employer didn't ask, "How many souls do you think you can win to Christ?" when they interviewed you, nor was it on the application. Some of us are not being true representatives of Christ. We are in someone else's place of employment trying to be preacher, evangelist or missionary extraordinaire when you're not fulfilling any of the requirements listed in your job description. The Bible says in **I Corinthians 14:40,** *"Let all things be done decently and in order."* Do what they *pay* you to do and the Lord will provide an opportunity to witness. However, when you really apply this scripture that's when you give God glory and people will be drawn in by your example.

Point 1: **Provide income for us to get the natural things we need.** Ecclesiastes 2:24 says, *"There is nothing better for a man, than that he should eat and drink, and that he should make his soul enjoy good in his labour. This also I saw, that it was from the hand of God."* Rather than complaining about the jobs we have or existing there with the wrong attitude we should as this scripture teaches enjoy good in our labor. In other words, thank God (it is from the hand of God) for the job you do have that helps you be responsible and puts food on the table. Go home each day knowing you have blessed God through your honest stewardship of that days work.

Point 2: **To reach the lost**. Acts 1:8 says, *"But you shall receive power, after that the Holy Ghost is come upon you: and ye shall* *be witnesses unto me both in Jerusalem, and in all Judea, and in Samaria, and unto the uttermost part of the earth."* We must have the power of God to be effective in the world we're living in. People need to be able to see us operating in the real power of God by dealing with every day situations, fears, adversities and conflicts. The Amplified Bible says it this way, *"But you shall receiver power, the ability, the efficiency and might."* What accurate wording for the workplace. After the power, the Holy Ghost is abiding in us, leading us, guiding us. Then we shall be witnesses. Most of us won't make it to Jerusalem, Judea or Samaria but we will be able to witness at the supermarket, in the computer store, at the bank, in school, in the restaurant, at the clothing shop, in the beauty salon or barber shop and thousands of workplaces. Remember, Jesus said, *"And I, If I be lifted up from the earth, will draw all men unto me."*

Point 3: **Establish disciplines/principles in our walk with God.** **Psalm 119:33-34** says, *"Teach me, O Lord, the way of thy statutes; and I shall keep it unto the end. Give me understanding, and I shall keep thy law; yea, I shall observe it with my whole heart."* What a lot of Believers lack is understanding and observance. Our places of work should be a place where we can put what we've learned in the sanctuary into practice. Again, and most important here, we are **_not_** talking about gifts but fruit. If you can live right at work you can live right anywhere. So many of us are even too ashamed to say we have accepted Christ as our Savior much less live like it. So you can't go to lunch with them, so you can't hang out on the dock with them, so you can't go to the office party, so you're outside of the loop? Do what you must but DON'T LOSE YOUR WITNESS. Don't let the enemy make a mockery of your life. Ask God to be with you, allow your spirit to keep you in tune with Him, be in this world but not OF this world. Ask the Lord daily to show you His ways but once He does be prepared to live them. It must be done with your whole heart. It can be done. The Lord wouldn't ask us if it weren't possible, *"Be ye holy for I <u>am</u> holy."* Live a disciplined/principled life before God and man wherever you work.

Point 4: **<u>Allow the light of the Lord to shine.</u>** Jesus said in **Matthew 5:16**, *"Let your light so shine before men, that they may see your good works, and glorify your Father which is in heaven."* <u>**Good works**</u>. Are you the one that's always late, always on the phone with personal calls, always making up a lie about your absence? Are you involved in office disputes? Do you gossip about co-workers or supervisors? Do they hear you cussing, see you smoking or acting unseemly? Are you chasing after the man or woman? God help us. Help us to get to a place where the world can see YOU through us. Meditate on this scripture. Make this one of your prayers before going to work. Do all you do to the glory of God and the next time someone asks you where do you work or what kind of work do you do, you can rest in knowing you *ARE* working for the Lord!

PRECEPT upon PRECEPT
LINE upon LINE

"GOD does not necessarily call the Equipped as much as HE EQUIPS THE CALLED!"

PRECEPT upon PRECEPT, LINE upon LINE

Everybody needs to understand how the Praise & Worship Team should function for proper alignment with the Word

This section is for the establishment, development and furtherance of Praise Teams worldwide. We will receive divine and practical insight of the functions within this body as well as directives in maintaining a God-led, Spirit-filled Worship unit.

AND THEY WERE ONE

II Chronicles 5:11-14

"And it came to pass, when the priests were come out of the holy **place:** *(for all the priests that were present were sanctified, and did not then wait by course:*

Also the Levites **which** *were the singers, all of them of Asaph, of Heman, of Jeduthun, with their sons and their brethren,* **being** *arrayed in white linen, having cymbals and psalteries and harps, stood at the east end of the altar, and them an hundred and twenty priests sounding with trumpets:)*

It came even to pass, as the trumpeters and singers were as one, to make one sound to be heard in praising and thanking the Lord; and when they lifted up **their** *voice with the trumpets and cymbals and instruments of musick, and praised the Lord,* **saying,** *For He is good; for His mercy* **endureth** *for ever: that* **then** *the house was filled with a cloud,* **even** *the house of the Lord;*

So that the priests could not stand to minister by reason of the cloud: for the glory of the Lord had filled the house of God."

Praise God for His Word. Look at this scripture carefully, Praise Team. The priests *came out* of the Holy of Holies <u>before</u> they took the people in. The priests that were used in *this* move of God had undergone purification rites. These priests of music and song were consecrated, prepared and unified – they were ONE; in their motive, in their agenda, in their purpose. When God knows He is the center of attention, the main attraction, the only star in the service, He moves in ways we have not known.

The Lord delights in our desire to please Him. Blessing Jesus is an honor no one should take for granted.

Knowing that He made me so I could touch Him is enough to find out how. Meditate on that…

"SOMEBODY NEEDS US!"

The Principles to Fulfill the Mandate

God has for the Praise & Worship Family

PRAYER – The foundation, the stabilizing factor behind/beneath every God-ordained ministry is prayer. You can not move forward and achieve the overall vision for this calling without prayer. Certainly prayer is the life-line, the security blanket and insurance policy for each need, concern and plan the Lord intends to accomplish. Prayer keeps you mindful of the sovereignty of God. Prayer keeps you dependent on God. Prayer allows you to hear from God and helps you stay focused on His purpose. Prayer is the act of communicating with the only source of strength, comfort and ultimate fulfillment.

"Pray without ceasing." **II Thessalonians 5:17**

"Don't worry about anything, pray about everything."
Philippians 4:6

PART COMPANY – Parting company is one of the things Believers find most difficult to do once called to a particular area of ministry. We must, as the Bible instructs us to, consecrate and go through the sanctification process if the Lord is going to use us effectively. The enemy seeks to keep us preoccupied with distractions of this world in order to keep our eyes off the things of God. Parting company takes on many variations, (i.e., lifestyles, relationships, attitudes, habits, misplaced traditions, etc.) but each and every one must be sacrificed on the altar of God in order to operate under the true anointing of God. God will never be able to use some of us until we trust Him enough to submit ALL.

"But your iniquities have separated between you and your God, and your sins have hid His face from you, that He will not hear."

Isaiah 59:2

"Wherefore come out from among them, and be ye separate, saith the Lord, and touch not the unclean thing; and I will receive you."

II Corinthians 6:17

"Blessed are ye, when men shall hate you, and when they shall separate you from their company, and shall reproach you and cast out your name as evil, for the Son of man's sake. Rejoice ye in that day, and leap for joy: for, behold, your reward is great in heaven..."

Luke 6:22-23 (a & b)

"Who shall separate us from the Love of Christ?"
Romans 8:35 (a)

Be a **PROTÉGÉ** – Webster's Dictionary says a protégé is a person guided and helped in his career (ministry) by another person. The principle person here is the Lord Jesus Christ. We must study the life He lived and learn daily the teachings and practices which God made available to us when His Son was made manifest in the flesh. Jesus is the primary and dominant example to everyone who desires to make a lifetime commitment to God the Father. In addition, we must take hold of your shepherd's leadership, vision and mission concerning your particular church body. Glean from them while serving. Ask the Lord to show you your pastor's burden for the people of God that you might be united in your ministry development.

"Then Jesus said unto His disciples, If any man will come after me, let him deny himself, and take up his cross, and follow me."

Matthew 16:24

"If any man serve me, let him follow me; and where I am, there shall also my servant be: if any man serve me, him will my Father honour." **John 12:26**

"Be ye therefore perfect (mature), even as your Father which is in Heaven is perfect"

Matthew 5:48

Get **PREGNANT** – In natural terms when a woman is pregnant she is carrying a life within her womb. From the moment of this joyous news, there's a great expectation. Immediate plans begin as they delight in the forthcoming event. Likewise, we the Praise & Worship Team must be "pregnant" with the Good News of Jesus. Our spirit should be alive with the truth and praises of God; excited about the endless possibilities when the Word of God is alive in you. This lets us know we have to study God's Word to know God. Pastors Harvey & Gloria Lewis have a saying, "How much do we know God? As much as we know His Word!" We can look forward to wonderful days ahead as we share the love of Christ that's within us. The church is anxious to receive the "Bundle of Praise" that He's birthed through you.

"He that believeth on me, as the scriptures hath said, out of his belly shall flow rivers of living water." **John 7:38**

"And God said, Let the waters bring forth abundantly the moving creature that hath life..." **Genesis 1:20(a)**

"Now unto him that is able to do exceeding abundantly above all that we ask or think, according to the power that worketh in us." **Ephesians 3:20**

Be a **PRAISE** – Praise is a state of being. That means you must now condition yourself in such a way that your very existence is a breath of fresh air to God. The prerequisite for Praise is breath. The Word says, ***"Let everything that has breath Praise God."*** When God seeks to be praised, He should be able to zero in on your life and find_____ (fill your name in here)_____, His Appointed Praiser. The devil needs to know when he is rushing in his efforts are in vain, insomuch as you and the Lord are already locked up in a relationship rooted in fervent prayer and praise. True praise will keep us from being preoccupied with the trials and tribulations of life. Most of all, Praise is a constant reminder of the goodness and greatness of God.

"I will praise thee, O Lord, with my whole heart; I will shew forth thy

marvelous works." **Psalms 9:1**

"Be thou exalted, Lord, in thine own strength: so will we sing and praise thy power." **Psalms 21:13**

"Rejoice in the Lord, O ye righteous: for praise is comely for the upright." **Psalm 33:1**

Be **PREPARED** – As a servant of God, we must stay *"at the ready"* concerning ministry work. So many have abused the callings of God by exploiting the purpose of that gift. Every good and perfect gift comes from God but we should remember it only comes to give God ALL the glory. Therefore, let us gird up our loins for this era of reconciliation, restoration and revival such as the world has never seen. As a servant you are going to be "on call" – 24/7; available and accessible to the Lord whenever He calls. Don't allow yourself to make your ministry a 'ministry of convenience' based on your schedule. Remembering the timing of God is always perfect. If the leadership sees a place for your ministry to be used, come running, without delay, quick, fast and in a great big hurry. There are souls at stake!

"And Samuel spoke unto all the house of Israel, saying, If ye do return unto the Lord with all your hearts, then put away the strange gods and Ash-ta-roth from among you, and prepare your hearts unto the Lord, and serve Him only: and He will deliver you out of the hand of the Philistines." **I Samuel 7:3**

"Even as the Son of man came not to be ministered unto, but to minister, and to give His life a ransom for many." **Matthew 20:28**

Stay in the **PRESENCE** of God – As we accept this spiritual challenge to hold the hand of the body of Christ and lead them to the place where the glory of God is found, we must dwell, bask, commune and live in His presence. How can you properly lead someone where you have never been? Let's say you're driving a friend to an unknown destination. You have directions written down, you may even have some idea of where you're going but for those who consider their time and effort precious they go ahead of time, so when the actual day comes they would have made themselves familiar with the route their taking. This is the same for the Praise & Worship Team, we should be familiar with the presence of God, if you don't know what it's like you will get lost trying to take someone else there. You can not ask someone to do what you don't do yourself. We must first lead by example, by experience, by knowledge but most of all by anointing. The true anointing that is as Pastor Dollar says, "The burden-removing, yoke-destroying power of God." In the Presence of God the Glory of God can be released.

As we seek to please the Lord we will rejoice in the <u>hope</u> of the glory of God!

> *"Cast me not away from thy presence;*
> *take not thy holy spirit from me."*
> **Psalm 51:11**

"Thou wilt shew me the path of life: in thy presence is fullness of joy; at thy right hand there are *pleasures for evermore."*
Psalm 16:11

"Now unto him that is able to keep you from falling, and to present you faultless before the presence of His glory with exceeding joy, To the only wise God our Saviour, be glory and majesty, dominion and power, both now and ever. Amen.
Jude 24-25

The T.E.A.M. Acronym

To operate under the power of the Holy Spirit, our Praise & Worship Family must understand what the Godly acronym for <u>TEAM</u> means:

TRAINED TO BE

EFFECTIVE

ANOINTED TO

MINISTER

Strengthened *to give* Strength,

Rejoicing *to share* Joy,

Blessed *to be* a Blessing!

WITHOUT ORDER
THERE WILL BE NO ANOINTING

Have you ever had or seen gold chain links start to snag? Sometimes they can snag in so many places it can not be worn anymore because it's so unattractive, not able to be used for its original intent which is to complement your overall appearance. This is how some of our Praise Teams are or more importantly *how we have <u>ALLOWED</u> them to become.* We have so many snags that we are an unsightly, broken up, worn out chain; not fit for God's use. (A snag is described as an unexpected or hidden difficulty, a complication, an obstacle, a problem.)

It's my sincere conviction that there must be order for the anointing to flow freely and continually. As a Praise Team member take self-inventory and ask, "Am I a snag? Am I one of the reasons there is not FULL order on our Team?" Whether you answer yes or no, all of us should be committed to growing and learning more about our responsibilities to Christ and the ministries we serve. Just think, we could be the cause of someone not experiencing the glory of God! How do we keep this from happening? **WE MUST OPERATE AS A TEAM!** Let this godly acronym for TEAM sink in your spirit:

TRAINED TO BE

EFFECTIVE

ANOINTED TO

MINISTER

TRAINED **T**O **B**E **E**FFECTIVE. I Chronicles 25:7 states, *"So the number of them, with their brethren that were instructed in the songs* *of the Lord, <u>even</u> all that were cunning."* We must be trained. We must receive instruction from the Word, from our pastors/leaders, from books, tapes, conferences and other resources made available for this vein of ministry but certainly we must not forget to be open to receive direct instruction from the Lord in our times of prayer and private worship. Proper instruction is a prerequisite for order. "…<u>even</u> all that were cunning." Cunning in this context means skillful. Each and every Praise Team member must be proficient in this area of service. I often hear Praise Teams' say, "We're doing the best we can with who we have." Who you have must be trained, they must be learned, and they must be taught – *properly*. Although to most church goers it just looks like a bunch of people standing up singing some songs, there is so much more that has to take place. The inner workings of your Team determines the outward results. If we are all trained we will have a positive lasting effect on the worship life of our church. But wait that's not all!

<u>ANOINTED TO MINISTER.</u> It is not until there is order the anointing can flow and consistent order ushers in a liberty God desires us to have. The Holy Spirit will not dwell in a disorganized, chaotic environment. So, once we've established order then we can seek the anointing. After we've done all we can in preparation to serve we know we are absolutely empty without the anointing. The Anointing, the power of God; an outpouring of God's Spirit to equip us for His service. Depend on the anointing. On our best days, our gifts can not meet the needs of God's people but the (trained) gift + the anointing will every time. Without God's help we are nothing but we can do all things through Christ that strengthens us. **Psalm 28:7-8** says, ***"The Lord is my strength and my shield; my heart trusted in Him, and I am helped: therefore my heart greatly rejoiceth; and with my song will I praise Him. The Lord is their strength and He is the saving strength of His anointed."*** We have been

called on to minister. Our trust is in the Lord, not ourselves, not our gifts and because we know He has promised to help us, we can rejoice and sing our song of Praise to Him with confidence in the living God. When life and service gets hard we know He will save us and strengthen us because of the anointing that lies within.

Dear Praise Team remember WITHOUT ORDER THERE WILL BE NO ANOINTING.

ATTRIBUTES of EFFECTIVENESS
for PRAISE & WORSHIP MINISTRY

We have received a mandate from God to offer a spiritually relevant and uplifting delivery each time we are called to serve. Here are some critical attributes every member of the Praise & Worship family should be developing daily:

LOVE	Mark 12:30-31	For God, your leaders, your co-laborers and for the mission of the ministry
FAITH	Philippians 1:6	In God; in His allowing you to serve in this sacred and joy-filled calling
AUTHORITY	Proverbs 28:1	This allows you to minister boldly at all times in every situation
HUMILITY	James 4:10	Never forgetting that it's ALL about GOD!
ATTITUDE	Romans 2:18-19	Of professionalism because we're serving God and His people with a spirit of excellence
MOTIVES	Philippians 3:13-15	Keeping God first which will keep you from misguided efforts, stagnation and imbalance
LOYALTY	Philippians 4:9	Let your allegiance be to God, when He's pleased all will be well

It's important to note the **vital purpose of PRAYER** to the maintenance of our spirit man as we practice these effective attributes.

IS THAT THE SAME MOUTH YOU USE
TO GIVE HIM PRAISE !?!

Scriptures can become so popular people rattle them off without any real understanding of what they just said. There is a degree of proclamation every time scripture is uttered. To proclaim means to declare publicly, insistently, proudly and formally. It also means to praise or glorify publicly. Praise Team, what you are using your mouth for privately could be hindering your declarations publicly. One of the most quoted scriptures by far is **Psalm 34:1**, *"I will bless the Lord at all times: His praise shall continually be in my mouth."* Don't you know Jesus is holding you accountable for every Word of Truth you declare? You may be operating subconsciously and only quoting scripture because it's the *one* you know or due to the weekly tradition at your church or to 'go with the flow' but each proclamation you speak has to be lived out – *by you*.

Read this carefully. **James 3:5-12 (**TLB**)**, *"So also the tongue is a small thing, but what enormous damage it can do. A great forest can be set on fire by one tiny spark. And the tongue is a flame of fire. It is full of wickedness, and poisons every part of the body. And the tongue is set on fire by hell itself, and can turn our whole lives into a blazing flame of destruction and disaster. Men have trained, or can train, every kind of animal or bird that lives and every kind of reptile or fish, but no human being can tame the tongue. It is always ready to pour out its deadly poison. Sometimes it praises our heavenly Father, and sometimes it breaks out into curses against men who are made like God. And so blessing and cursing come pouring out of the same mouth. Dear brothers, surely this is not right! Does a spring of water bubble out first with fresh water and then with bitter water? Can you pick olives from a fig tree or figs from a grapevine? No, and you can't draw fresh water from a salty pool."*

There are six (6) specific offenses of the tongue we need to be aware of:

1) **A Complaining Tongue.** *"Teach me, and I will hold my tongue."* (Job 6:24a) Before your thoughts get to your mouth and causes you to start blaming and complaining, pray this prayer from Job. Teach me Lord to see your sovereignty in my day-to-day situation knowing all things work together for good to them that love You and are called according to Your purpose.

2) **A Gossiping Tongue.** *"Lord who shall abide in thy tabernacle? Who shall dwell in thy holy hill? He that backbiteth not with his tongue, nor doeth evil to his neighbor, nor taketh up a reproach against his neighbor."* (Psalm 15:1 & 3) There is a promise made here to those that do not partake in destroying another's life with words – you can rest in the place where the Lord is, you can live on the hills of holiness and faith.

3) **A Lying Tongue.** *"These [six] things doth the Lord hate. A proud look, a lying tongue, and hands that shed innocent blood."* (Proverbs 6:16a-17a) Take special note of anything the Lord hates, this lets us know He deals heavily with these issues. Surrender – even your excuse of necessity, your imagination and your justification of any lie – to Jesus. He will build you up in truth.

4) **A Profane Tongue.** *"But shun profane and vain babblings: for they will increase unto more ungodliness."* (II Timothy 2:16) The curse words, the filthiness, the haughtiness that comes from the carnal tongue will eventually lead you further and further away from Godly behavior. Keep it clean, keep it holy.

5) **A C̲u̲r̲s̲i̲n̲g̲ T̲o̲n̲g̲u̲e̲.** *"For their tongues aim lies like poisoned spears. They speak cleverly to their neighbors while planning to kill them."* (Jeremiah 9:8) God help us, what treachery! Let us not be found guilty of this. Let every word be governed by the convicting power of the Holy Spirit.

6) **A D̲e̲a̲t̲h̲ T̲o̲n̲g̲u̲e̲.** *"Death and life are in the power of the tongue: and they that love it shall eat the fruit thereof."* (Proverbs 18:21) Whatever you chose to speak will be life-giving or life-altering. <u>Before</u> you speak, listen to what's flowing through your spirit. If it's negative, arrest and correct that thought with the Word of God. If your thought is the will of God, embrace it and proclaim it. What you speak can make all the difference between victory and defeat.

Please pray the Lord will search your heart concerning how you use your instrument – the tongue. Let us pray the words of David in his time of brokenness, ***"Deliver me from bloodguiltiness, O God, thou God of my salvation: and my tongue shall sing aloud of thy righteousness. O Lord, open thou my lips; and my mouth shall shew forth thy praise."*** Praise Team let us honor the Lord always…

A COMMITMENT TO STUDY

II Timothy 2:15

"Study to shew thyself approved unto God, a workman that needeth not to be ashamed, rightly dividing the word of truth." (KJV)

"Work hard so God can say to you, "Well done." Be a good workman, one who does not need to be ashamed when God examines your work.

Know what His word says and means." (TLB)

"Study and be eager and do your utmost to present yourself to God approved (tested by trial), a workman who has no cause to be ashamed, correctly analyzing and accurately dividing [rightly handling and skillfully teaching] the Word of Truth." (TAB)

This scripture is critical to the spiritual success of every Praise Team member. How many Praise Team members do you know that do not come to Bible Study...ever? Or, they've been in Bible Study but when the course ended so did their limited knowledge of God's Word. How many of us sit in the remainder of the service after a wonderful time of Praise & Worship and daydream while pastors strive to deliver the unadulterated Word of God? How many of us have had a church member ask us a question concerning the Bible or the song we sang and we in turn made up an answer due to lack of knowledge? Looking deep doesn't make us deep. Acting deep doesn't make you deep. Knowing every praise song doesn't make us a true praiser. Let's face it; many people are missing the Lord right in the church. Why? We don't know God. How can we represent someone we don't know ourselves? I mean know in a real way; in an unwavering way, in such a way that we as the worship family can be put on assignment to secure victory in every battle. It is possible but first, <u>know the Word</u>. We must be doers and not just hearers of the Word.

Our focus scripture in all translations emphasizes the need to be approved by God. Some of us are serving people but not God. He is the author and finisher of our faith. He is the One I long to get a yes from, a nod of approval, a smile of reassurance. Everyone else may have a blank expression or a disapproving look but if the *Son* is shining down on me, I know I can do all things.

As a Praise & Worship Team member, a 'Commitment to Study' is established and maintained when the following three disciplines become priority.

1) **STUDY HIS WORD.**

   Study – to examine thoroughly so as to understand and interpret. How can we know God unless we know His Word? Get hungry, stay hungry for the Word. Don't just partake in the Word when someone else is preaching or teaching; get to know the Lord for yourself. Live in the Word. Learn the Word. Love the Word. Look to the Word. Lack of knowledge will cause us to perish. You want a life of holiness, it's in the Word. You want a vibrant, thriving ministry, it's in the Word. You want proper instruction and direction, it's in the Word. Study God's Word.

2) **STUDY HIS PRESENCE.**

   Study – to ascertain and act in accordance with. You've got to know what it is to be in the presence of God; the difference between the Outer Court, Inner Court and Holy of Holies. What God wants and how to respond to

Him at each stage of development in His presence. God desires to reveal Himself to us so we can reveal Him to someone else – what a blessed honor! As the Amplified Bible says, "we must rightly handle and skillfully teach" based on the truth of God's Word what He requires of His people when we come before Him. How can we take someone where we have never been? You should be able to assist your worship leader in guiding your congregation to God's appointed destination for each service.

3) **STUDY HIS GIFT TO YOU**.

Study – to aim at achieving, an earnest endeavor. All of us should seek to get the most out of the gift(s) God has given us. Why are you singing soprano when you should be singing tenor. You're hurting the gift and our ears. Why are you singing alto when the sopranos need you desperately, you're just slothful and lazy. Why are you subjecting the church to a song you wrote that the Lord meant for you to keep private? How come you don't know what you're able to do naturally as well as under the anointing? There *is* a difference. As a Praise Team member, the ability to raise your hands and dance before God is the enhancement of your vocal gift. Singing, "I will dance as David danced" and never actually dancing is a contradiction. Study His gift to you in its totality and endeavor to get the most out of it. Honor God by developing your gift properly.

I am 'Committed to Study'…are you!?!

A VISUAL TRANSFORMATION:
From Stage Presence to 'PRAISE' Presence

Praise Team members imagine yourself walking to the spot where you lead God's people into Praise and Worship but wait…see yourself *from* the congregation. What do you see?

There is one of two extremes so many Team members fit under according to most congregations: 1) Either they are so caught up in themselves they have mastered all the professional motions, facial expressions and hand movements, (some of us study secular artists to see what they're doing). Or, 2) They have not yet gained spiritual confidence and appear to be lacking the conviction, joy, intent and power necessary to minister to anyone.

The first three years (the foundational years) of our Praise Team, I had many people to make comments like the following, "You all are such a blessing but…That young man must really think he's something! Does that young woman ever smile? So and so had an attitude today." Even with the anointing present, even with a move of the Spirit, even with growth in our presentation, I still had to weigh those comments and in some instances convey those concerns to the Praise Team. Why? Because we must be aware of ourselves visually as much as we are spiritually and vocally.

The enemy will use whatever he can to distract us from experiencing the presence of God. Your whole Team could be shouting for joy but someone will come and say, "_____ never dances for the Lord, do they?" This is why it's so crucial we make a concentrated effort to change our stage presence into PRAISE presence. Someone is watching you. And while we are not performers, we should be an expression of God through the life of a genuine praiser. Let's think about it a moment: What do they see? Are they persuaded to bless God? Do they feel compelled to give the Lord high praise? Do they get to the point in the intimacy of worship that they can go beyond you? Or are they so impressed/depressed with the way you look they can't even see God? Is your personae pulling down strongholds or blocking the view of seeing Jesus?

As I go from place to place and meet Praise Teams of every denomination I notice certain similarities. Lack of PRAISE presence is one of them. Look at the scriptures, *"So we thy people and sheep of thy pasture will give thee thanks for ever: we will shew forth thy praise to all generations."* (**Psalm 79:13**) *"O Magnify the Lord with me, and let us exalt His name together."* (**Psalm 34:3**) *"O come, let us sing unto the Lord: let us make a joyful noise to the rock of our salvation. O come, let us worship and bow down; let us kneel before the Lord our maker."* (**Psalm 95:1&6**) What do these verse have in common – ACTS OF CORPORATE PRAISE!!! Our Teams have to band together (each and every one of us) to make these scriptures come to life in our churches. No loose ends. No individual hindrances. Yes, all of us have our own ways of expressing praise but <u>*everyone*</u> should be praising God with all that is within. The congregation will have no choice but to join your Team in giving God what He deserves – the best, most sincere praise we have, at all times. There is no limit to the heights and depths we will experience in God if we commit to His Word which says, *"But ye are a chosen generation, a royal priesthood, an holy nation, a peculiar people; that should shew forth the praises of Him who hath called you out of darkness into His marvelous light."* (**I Peter 2:9**) When we transform our stage presence into **PRAISE PRESENCE, God** *inhabits our* **PRAISE** and **we** *enjoy* **HIS PRESENCE.**

I MUST SING the LORD'S SONG

"Can your Song be Sung at the <u>THRONE</u> or just here on earth?"

"WHAT KIND OF SONG ARE YOU SINGING?"

It has become terribly burdensome to me how the church has allowed the world to infiltrate and contaminate the pure essence of the song of the Lord. From vocal lines to instrumental arrangements we have desecrated our time of Song wherein there is no hope for the flow of the anointing to permeate the atmosphere placing us at the feet of Jesus. We desperately need to get back to exalting the Most High God and join heaven in a continuous chorus of true Praise. The structure for cultivating a repertoire that honors God is as follows:

I. **WHERE DOES A SONG COME FROM?**

   A. The creativity of God

   1. James 1:17 – *"Every good and perfect gift is from above, and cometh down from the Father of lights, with whom is no variableness, neither shadow of turning."*

   B. Obedience through the voice and direction of God

   1. Psalms 119:54 – *"Thy statutes (law or ordinance) have been my songs in the house of my pilgrimage."*

   C. Your walk, your faith, your relationship, an experience, a tragedy, a triumph…

   1. Many have sung before us. *Some of our most cherished hymns were written from the life of one who had experienced and survived unbelievable situations because of the grace of God.*

II. **MAN'S EXPLOITATION (and downright abuse) OF THE GIFT OF SONG**

   A. **The devil's influence and use of song**

   1. He was the Chief musician / Head songwriter

   2. Jealous of any song that glorifies God

   B. **Selfish gain for a sacred gift**

   1. The world entices you with material gain, power of popularity

   2. The "saints" – starring on God's time

   3. Entertainment vs. Conviction

      a. Ezekiel 33:32 (TLB) – *"You are very entertaining to them, like someone who sings lovely songs with a beautiful voice or plays well on an instrument. They hear what you say but don't pay any attention to it."*

      b. Acts 16:25-26 – *"And at midnight Paul and Silas prayed, and sang praise unto God: and the prisoners heard them. And suddenly there was a great earthquake, so that the foundations of the prison were shaken: and immediately all the doors were opened, and every one's bands were loosed."*

III. **THE ACCEPTABLE SONG**

   A. Found in the Word

   B. What kind?

1. Ephesians 5:19 – *"Speaking to yourselves in psalms, hymns and spiritual songs, singing and making melody in your heart to the Lord."*

    a. Your personal song-life

    b. Everyone of us has a song

2. Colossians 3:16 – *"Let the word of Christ dwell in you richly in all wisdom; teaching and admonishing one another in psalms, hymns and spiritual songs, singing with grace in your hearts to the Lord."*

    a. Edification to the Body of Christ

    b. Tehillah – a corporate song

C. What style?

1. Psalms – scriptures set to music

2. Hymns – anthems of the Church

3. Spiritual Songs – songs received, sung and quickened by the Holy Spirit

4. The standard by which to judge a song of God

    a. Philippians 4:4* – *"Whatsoever things are true, whatsoever things are honest, whatsoever things are just, whatsoever things are pure, whatsoever things are lovely, whatsoever things are of good report; if there be any virtue, and if there be any praise, think on these things."* (*In this scripture please replace the *things* with song.)

b. Satisfying the spirit rather than the flesh

- The priority of wanting His presence should override your need to satisfy your musical/song preference – style, tempo, instrumentation, etc. As long as His presence is not the overwhelming factor, your flesh will demand to be satisfied.

D. Is it seasonal or eternal?

1. Know whether a song is meant to be sung through a particular season or move of God. Example: *"This is the year of the Open Door"*

2. Learn how to acknowledge a song that will live throughout eternity. Example: "Great is Thy Faithfulness". These songs normally speak of the eternal magnificence of God.

IV. EVERY SONG OF GOD SHOULD END GIVING ALL GLORY TO GOD!!!

GUIDELINES FOR PRAISE & WORSHIP SONG SELECTION

1. *Each and every song on your repertoire must be scripturally sound.*

2. A song must either glorify God, edify believers or persuade unbelievers to Christ Jesus.

3. Psalms, Hymns and Spiritual Songs which includes a wide variation of song styles should be the basis of a solid, thorough repertoire. (*Ephesians 5:19 and Colossians 3:16*)

4. The majority of your songs should be simple and easy enough for the congregation to pick up almost immediately, with very few exceptions, (such as event type songs: Christmas or Easter; songs requested by the Pastor; feature praise songs which they will eventually learn after hearing a few times).

5. Difficult vocal passages or moves should not be tried unless they are appropriate for the group singing them and have been properly rehearsed, so as not to interrupt the flow of the praise and worship service.

6. No song should depend on loud accompaniment to get through or touch the people. The people of God should not sing based on what they're made to feel but what they know.

7. While it is you must remain open to the Holy Spirit, you must also conquer the fear of giving the people only the songs they're familiar with and readily accept. God sent a specific assignment to the P&W Family, "*Sing unto the Lord a NEW song.*"

A FRESH REVELATION for a STANDARD PRINCIPLE

If you are a worship leader then you know one of the most difficult task in your service to God is, "Singing A New Song." Sounds easy enough doesn't it but unlike our cousins in the music ecclesia, 'The Choir', we not only have to sing a new song but we must encourage the congregation to *join* us in singing that new song. Too many of us have allowed the praise & worship segment of our service to become a time of spectating rather than a time for participating. Our churches are looking and listening but not learning to offer songs of praise to God corporately. The Hebrew word of Praise we apply here is, ***TEHILLAH*** *which means to sing and glorify the Lord.* **To sing in the spirit brings tremendous unity to those who are worshipping together and once you experience the impact this has you will understand how critical it is to get/keep the congregation involved – from beginning to end. And while it is the people may seem to be blessed more when they know the song you're singing we can not ignore the command of God to SING A NEW SONG.**

I've been taught by the Spirit that anything in the Word of God which is repeated denotes importance. 'Sing unto the Lord a new Song' is stated five (5) times in the Bible (***Psalms 33:3, 96:1, 149:1 and Isaiah 42:10***) and on four (4) other occasions the issue of a new song being sung is highlighted in the text (***Psalms 40:3, 144:9, Revelation 5:9, 14:3***). The Psalms are considered to be the Songbook of the Bible and our (Worship Leaders) instruction manual. Our gifts are enhanced; our worship is consistently effective when we obey the instructions given to us by God. When I meet with pastors and in private settings with the church assembly, two of the most frequent complaints is the Praise Team does NOT sing any new songs or either (believe it or not) they DO NOT LIKE the new songs the Praise Team is singing, which frightens most worship leaders. I'm sure you've had to deal with both of these issues at some point as I have or you may be dealing with them right now but the Lord won't leave you by yourself. The Holy Spirit will provide the help you need to fulfill God's request.

In my research and fellowship with different denominations I have learned Baptist, Methodist and Episcopal settings tend to prefer hymns and anthems. Pentecostals tend to lean towards more jubilant praise songs and ole' time church material. Charismatic aggregations seem to like an abundance of Worship-oriented songs. (However, I do feel real Praise and true Worship songs are on the upswing in most churches regardless of denomination because people are seeking God in a greater way and those songs are a sincere expression of their desire to love and please God). Whatever the case may be, in His command to sing a new song God didn't say what *style* of songs. The most specific He got was telling Apostle Paul to tell us to sing making melody and to sing with grace in our hearts to the Lord with Psalms, Hymns and Spiritual Songs (**Ephesians 5:19** and **Colossians 3:16**). If the song is *from* God, it will bless God and bless us too. The message God wants conveyed should be the primary concern in your choice of songs. Style is a matter of taste, of background, of what you've been exposed to, but we should not limit the potential for our church to gain access into the Holy of Holies based on style. That's a mere technicality. Dr. Thomas Dorsey suffered so much criticism from the church when he introduced "Precious Lord" because it was different from what the church was used to hearing but NOW it is one of the world's most loved hymns. We have to be open to a fresh move of God. We have to teach God's people to sing a new song.

What song God is calling for in that *particular Worship gathering* is the real issue. There may be a place God is trying to take your congregation to but you have not sung the song yet. Think of the possibilities…

Worship leaders we need to break this stronghold by the power of God. But how do we begin? How do we overcome this obstacle that hinders us from allowing God to operate in an atmosphere of liberty? The following are scriptural practices that will help to destroy some insecurities the enemy uses to keep us from going deeper in Christ:

> A. *"He brought me up also out of an horrible pit, out of the miry clay, and set my feet upon a rock, and established my goings. And <u>He hath put a new song in my mouth</u>, even praise unto our God; many shall see it, and fear, and shall trust in the Lord."* (**Psalms 40:2-3**) This scripture says so much. He saved me, gave me security and placed me in the center of His will for my life. And now I have to sing about it. A song God Himself gave me, a song I have not sung before, a song that comes from relationship; a song that leads to a greater praise, a deeper worship. And as a result, souls will see the goodness of God, they will reverence Him and be confident in knowing the Lord is able.
>
> B. *"Praise ye the Lord. Sing unto the Lord a new song, and His praise in the congregation of saints."* (**Psalms 149:1**) It should be obvious by now God delights in His people offering a new song. We know God inhabits the praises of His people, so then the combination of praises and spirit-filled songs must be His 'rest stop.' Not only are we fulfilling a command when we sing a new song but we are loving God in a very special way.

C. *"O sing unto the Lord a new song; for He hath done marvelous things: His right hand, and His holy arm, hath gotten Him the victory."* (**Psalms 98:1**) The Lord loves for us to give our gifts back to Him as they speak of His awesome majesty. The gift of song is marvelous in and of itself whether you are a singer, songwriter or musician. When it serves the purpose for which it was intended – to glorify God, I believe that releases a special anointing to meet the need of everyone present and opens the way for God to pour out His Spirit to show us His glory as we have ever seen.

Men and Women of Praise, it is my prayer you gain courage to go forth in this delicate area of our ministry. Do not be intimidated by your environment. Let God lead you and everyone present into a place of fulfillment through the obedience of His Word. He can't wait to hear you sing a NEW song!

THE CONCLUSION

"Let us hear the conclusion of the whole matter: Fear God, and keep His commandments: for this is the whole duty of man." Ecclesiastes 12:13

I DON'T NEED ANY PROOF
YOUR WORD IS ENOUGH FOR ME!

These are the times that try men's souls. I've been hearing that phrase since I was a little girl but it has never been more real than it is now, especially for Believers. Like many of our fore mothers and fathers in the Bible those of us who walk with God are being directed by the Holy Spirit to walk by faith and not sight. God gives us a word – in payer time, our worship, while reading/studying the Word, in a message and so many other hundreds of ways. However, before that Word can take root in your spirit the enemy wants you to reject it *before* the manifestation. Reject it how? Primarily through <u>unbelief</u>. Some of us need to pray right now, *Lord, I believe; help thou mine unbelief.* There is a part of you that believes only in the moment of the promise but what happens when we leave the protective tenderness of that moment and go back to the harshness of reality? We lose faith, we lose hope, and we lose focus.

The Amplified Bible, **Hebrew 11:1** says, *"Now faith is the assurance (the confirmation, the title deed) of the things [we] hope for, being the proof of things [we] do not see and the conviction of their reality [faith perceiving as real fact what is not revealed to the senses]."* This says faith is the assurance. Assurance is a guarantee, a promise, a word, a certainty, a surety! Although everything around us says the exact opposite. I don't know what your particular promise is nor do I know your situation but you better believe the minute the devil gets the news (because he has to be informed, he is not omniscient) he gets to work trying to discredit the Word of the Lord. Remember, he is the father of lies; a master deceiver. ***He comes but for to kill, steal and destroy*** every promise God will ever give you. Don't forget, your faith is the title deed, it means by *faith* I already own the promise. I have the authority to claim that which God has promised me. I will live in the conviction of that promise and with confidence the promise became tangible the minute God spoke it. Don't let Satan fool you, he wants to steal your joy while you're living in expectation of the promise. Saints, where is our faith??? It's a MUST! Satan knows that your faith will please God. *"But without faith it is impossible to please Him: for he that cometh to God must believe that He is, and that He is a rewarder of them that diligently seek Him."* The report we're getting in the natural says it's absolutely impossible. That promise seems impossible sometimes (most of the time) doesn't it? Do as the scripture says, if you're coming to God you must believe that He is able to do the impossible. Your faith can not be based on anything in the natural, not you, not who you know or any other natural factor.

One of the reasons the enemy is so successful at discouraging us is because we sometimes get too far from God and those reminders of the promise. God knows we're human and He will often send confirmation but we shouldn't need daily updates of confirmation to begin to praise God in advance for the promise *alone*. God, You said I was going to be promoted but I just got fired – hold on to the promise. You said You would bring closure to my situation but all hell is breaking loose – hold on to the promise. I don't need proof, Your WORD is enough for me. Hallelujah!!!

Faith comes by hearing and hearing by the Word of God. God knew we would need the security and reassurance of His Word along with the witness through the Holy Spirit that His promises are yea and amen!

Let's make the devil a liar. Go ahead, dig your promise out of that closet you buried it in, renew your faith and trust in the Almighty God. Get that promise at the forefront of your mind and spirit right now; and without any evidence, any proof and any change in your circumstances say to God – I don't need any proof, your WORD is enough for me! Hallelujah, Your WORD is enough for me! Thank you Jesus, Your WORD is enough for me! **Lord, I know You're able and Your WORD is enough for me! Glory to God!**

EXPECT NOTHING BUT VICTORY!!!

"For the Lord God is a sun and shield: the Lord will give grace and glory: no good thing will He withhold from them that walk uprightly. O Lord of hosts, blessed is the man that trusteth in Thee." (**Psalms 84:11-12**)

Look up and live! The Savior of our souls is leading us to the light of His glory. This scripture is conditional, it speaks to those that are in relationship with the Lord, "...*them that walk uprightly.*" I love this passage of the Word and I've experienced the revelation of its magnitude during some of the most difficult days I've ever seen.

Look carefully, **"For the Lord God is a sun and shield..."** When times have been darkest and the enemy sought to overtake me – <u>there God is</u>! *"...the Lord will give grace and glory..."* When I'm being overwhelmed by the hardness of life or by the solicitation for compromise in a Godless generation – <u>my God will</u>! Notice the scripture is written in the present tense, **is/will**, which means whenever His children, His beloved need Him the most He's already being God.

"No good thing will He withhold..." Whatever it is you're longing for and waiting for understand this, if it's good (God's best) for you He will not hold it back but if it's not in His perfect will for you, He will not release anything to you that will be harmful now or in the future. Walking upright is a must here, you will not use God. There are similar scriptures to support this conditional promise, *"Delight thyself also in the Lord; and He shall give thee the desires of thine heart."* (**Psalms 37:4**) *"But without faith it is impossible to please Him: for He that cometh to God must believe that He is, and that He is a rewarder of them that diligently seek Him."* (**Hebrews 11:6**) *"But seek ye first the kingdom of God and His righteousness; and all*

these things shall be added unto you." (**Matthew 6:33**) He's looking for Worshippers. He knows when you are completely satisfied with Him only. Learn to enjoy the privilege, honor and tremendous fulfillment of loving Him. Rebuke any hidden motives; stop hurting God by pretending to be His and start being real; you'll surprise yourself and fall in love with God deeply and you won't take nothing for the joy He gives. You will be in awe of His magnificent love and grace. *For those in true relationship, you know what I'm speaking of.*

Some people lose focus because things don't come together like they think they should or within the time they think but we have to go further, ***"O Lord of hosts, blessed is the man that trusteth in Thee."*** You must trust God. Don't let His sovereignty scare you but rather, let it give you security. Let Him do what He wants when He wants, how He wants, where He wants, with whom He wants, ***"knowing that all things work together for good to them that love Him and are called according to His purpose"*** – again, we're talking about relationship. A key element for peace while He's working and the promise being fulfilled, because He knows you and loves the way *you* love Him.

Learn how to flow with Him and not against Him and you can expect nothing but victory. ***"But thanks be to God, which giveth us the victory through our Lord Jesus Christ."*** You must have Christ, to have victory. You may win a battle or two being in an environment of salvation because Christ has conquered our enemy but come up higher and be secure in the knowledge and truth of His Word – daily. Refuse to live in fear or question the outcome of your trials by believing the promises of His Word.

Worshippers, Lovers of God, Diligent Seekers – **Expect Nothing but VICTORY!!!**

For Power, Strategies and a refreshing approach to Success, get Dr. Nelson's groundbreaking book:

Featured on www.pastorcee.today / www.amazon.com

WriteHouse is a Full Service Publishing Company:
We make YOUR goal to publish DOABLE.

www.writehousepublishing.com

Remember,
only what you do
for <u>CHRIST</u> will last.

www.ingramcontent.com/pod-product-compliance
Lightning Source LLC
Chambersburg PA
CBHW070817100426
42742CB00012B/2382